SUPER
CALLANETICS

THE
ADVANCED EXERCISE
PROGRAMME

Also by Callan Pinckney:

Callanetics
Callanetics for Your Back
Callanetics Countdown

Dedication

To Edwina Sandys.
How I have enjoyed tremendously all the wonderful laughs we have had
throughout the years.
Thank you.

Acknowledgments

I love every minute of preparing books and videos that will help people get stronger and shapelier. It is a complicated process that always requires a strong support group.

I would like to extend very special thanks to Gail Rebuck and Amelia Thorpe of the Random Century Group, who have published my books with such verve and enthusiasm for the past several years; to my attorney, Marc Bailin, and my agent, Mitch Douglas—and finally, to all of the wonderful people around the world who do Callanetics and Super Callanetics; and especially to those who have written to me about how my programs have improved their bodies and given them self-confidence.

A Note of Warning

Do not *ever* attempt to do any of the Super Callanetics exercises until you are completely familiar and comfortable with the Callanetics philosophy, movements, exercises, and terminology.

You *must* have completed and mastered at least ten hours of the one-hour Callanetics program before attempting *any* of these exercises.

There are risks inherent in any exercise program. The advice of a physician should be obtained prior to embarking upon a rigorous exercise program like Super Callanetics. This program is intended for people in good health who have already mastered the one-hour Callanetics program.

If you are pregnant, these advanced Super Callanetics exercises are *not* suitable.

A Note About the Neck

By this time, after having completed at least ten hours of the one-hour Callanetics program, you should feel nothing in your neck except for a lovely, wonderful stretch.

But because most people are not trained (or able!) to relax, your neck and/or upper back may ache the first time you do the stomach exercises. If so, you can support your neck by clasping your hands lightly around it, with your elbows pointed out to the side. Always keep your neck relaxed during these exercises.

If you still feel pain at the back of your neck after you have completed at least ten hours of the one-hour program, consult your physician.

A Note About Knee Problems

Callanetics has helped many people strengthen their knees and relieve chronic pain. If you have severe knee problems, do these exercises only with the consent of your physician.

A Note About Back Problems

Callanetics has also helped thousands of people relieve their back problems. However, it is advisable to use discretion when doing Super Callanetics if you have any back problems. If you have any history of backaches or other physical complaints, you should consult a physician before attempting these, or any other, exercises.

Sciatica Syndrome and Other Chronic Problems

You will notice that some of the exercises have notes about what to do if you have sciatica. Please follow these instructions carefully.

If, however, your sciatica or any other condition continues to give you discomfort and seems to have been aggravated by any of these exercises, discontinue doing them.

Three Professionals' Reactions
to Doing Callan's Program

Now, I consider myself to be in excellent shape, but she put me through a workout that had me very surprised about my own athletic strength . . . it was an incredible experience.

ALBERT BIANCHINE
A Professional Ski Instructor

I felt a lot more confident about my body. It got much stronger, and this helped free up my breathing. I feel like the notes are just flowing right out . . . .

ANN WHITNEY
Singer

The (Program) not only shaped my buttocks, but it helped the muscles a ballet dancer uses to "turn out" into position, and because my legs became so much stronger, I found I could leap higher.

CINDY BENNETT
Dancer

CONTENTS

BUTTOCKS—OUTER THIGHS—HIPS
Page 101

THE ENTIRE BODY
Page 121

STRETCHES
Page 127

PELVIS—FRONT AND INNER THIGHS
Page 141

THE TWENTY-MINUTE SUPER CALLANETICS ROUTINE
Page 155

Why Super Callanetics?

One day, back when I began teaching Callanetics in the early seventies, a student of mine was working hard during a class. Suddenly, she turned to me—and I remember that when she first started doing Callanetics, she'd had really soft, gooshy buttocks, and her body was very weak—and she said, 'Callan, this is getting too easy. I don't feel anything!'

I realized I felt exactly the same way.

I wanted to feel more, that wonderful sensation of the muscles working deep that is the basis for all the Callanetics and Super Callanetics exercises. Not only that, but my students wanted more of a challenge; they were getting so tight and so strong, so quickly, that I needed to take them further. (And most of these students were people like you and me—who despise exercising, and who will sometimes look for excuses not to spend an hour shaping their bodies. Sometimes I think that exercising is worse than washing your hair. And sometimes I'd rather plow a field . . . but I don't live near a field and where do you get a mule and, besides, I don't know how to plow . . . so I end up scrubbing between the kitchen tiles with a toothbrush!)

That's when I began to develop what has become Super Callanetics.

It's human nature, of course, to get lazy about whatever it is you're doing—work, play, sports, even relationships—once you become really good at it. And when I found myself getting very nonchalant because the one-hour Callanetics program had become too easy, I slowly began to develop a new and more intense version of the familiar Callanetics exercises—Super Callanetics. I wanted to get the same fast results in an even shorter amount of time. At first, I wasn't even certain that I would succeed, but I did already know that after your body becomes stronger from doing the one-hour Callanetics program, you'll have found that you can do the same amount of exercises in a shorter amount of time. Would the same principle apply to Super Callanetics? The answer, of course, is yes. Some of the movements may look the same as the basic ones—but when it comes to Super Callanetics, looks can be very deceiving.

What Super Callanetics Can Do for You

Several years ago, I was invited to West Berlin to teach Callanetics to some of the American Green Beret and Special Forces soldiers stationed there. Before I began their training, I was more than happy to teach some of the other soldiers on the base—particularly those from other countries who were competing in different sports—who were interested in Callanetics. There was one in particular, an expert in martial arts from Britain's Royal Air Force, who really was a lovely chap. He watched me demonstrate Callanetics with intense interest. 'God, this is *incredible*,' he said in his lovely clipped accent. 'It doesn't seem like you're doing *anything*. You're not even *moving*!'

I laughed. 'That's the whole point! Less *is* sometimes better,' I said. 'If you talk to most of the chaps stationed here, you'll find that many of them are suffering from back problems, and the reason is that they've never been taught to isolate their muscles, or how to relax. And when people can't relax and their bodies are tense all the time from using muscles they don't need to use, they wind up wasting all their energy, and wearing themselves out.'

His eyes grew wider. 'I can't *believe* you said that,' he exclaimed. 'You are so right! I've always believed that was true, but no one would listen to me. And I know it's got to be correct, because I've taught myself how to relax, and where the results really show are in competition. One of the

15

reasons I'm so good is that I can outlast my competitors, because now I know how to save my energy by *relaxing,* and only concentrating on the muscles that are working.'

His enthusiasm was infectious. Because, frankly, he was the only person I've *ever* run into who totally understood what I was saying without having experienced Super Callanetics or even the one-hour Callanetics program. The one-hour program was so revolutionary when it was first developed that even the doctors I talked to looked at me as if I were some kind of female Tarzan, still living in the deepest jungle. Now, of course, many of the same doctors who pooh-poohed Callanetics not only recommend it to their patients but recommend Super Callanetics as well. The original Callanetics program was designed to alleviate my personal medical problems. At the time, some of what I was saying seemed positively revolutionary. But the various Callanetics routines have always been based on nothing more complicated than common sense. I first began developing Callanetics, as you may know by now, because my bad back and knees were get-

ting worse—and they certainly weren't helped by what they experienced when I took exercise classes. Some of the movements I was allegedly 'taught' in these classes were so violent that they became the final straw of abuse my body could take. I feared I would be spending the rest of my life in a wheelchair. Thankfully, I have been able to put those fears to rest.

And I would also just like to tell you one more little thing about those Green Berets and Special Forces soldiers in Berlin. Growing up with Hollywood movies as I did, I always rather expected these soldiers to be brawny and indefatigable, the most physically fit people in the world. They were so funny at first—they wanted to know why the general had sent someone like me, who barely came up to most of their chests, to teach them these Tinkerbell exercises. And then they found they couldn't even do twenty Open and Closes, which is an exercise some seventy-five-year-old men and women can do in a breeze once they've built up their muscle strength. (I must confess that this made me a teeny bit nervous, because these are supposed to be the men whose job it is to protect people like me against our enemies!) Those soldiers certainly ate their words after a few Callanetics sessions . . . especially when their backaches went away.

You don't have to be a soldier or a fitness fanatic to do Super Callanetics. It can work for you, because it's you working your own muscles at your own pace. There are no weights involved, no use of any pressure on your body other than what your own muscles can do. Super Callanetics allows people of any age and ability to feel and look so much better, without fear of exhaustion or injury. It does not take years, as it does with ballet or yoga, to become proficient in Super Callanetics. And it only takes an hour or two a week or a few minutes a day for you to see some truly amazing results.

I am also certain that by now you have noticed not only a transformation of your body, but a lovely feeling of self-confidence that comes with learning how to be in control. That is because Callanetics and Super Callanetics are like meditation in motion.

Think of how delightful it is to take a vacation in Ibiza or Greece or a Caribbean island, to lie in the relaxing heat, listening to the soothing waves of the ocean—not from a headset!—or watching a glorious sunset, and then sitting blissfully underneath the spectacle of millions of stars glowing in a clear night sky (if you're fortunate enough to be somewhere with no pollution). That lovely feeling of relaxation, of flowing, of being soothed by the sound of the ocean . . . combined with the wonderful knowledge that you *can* be in control of your body, is what I want Super Callanetics to be for you. (To say nothing of how marvelous you will wind up looking in your bathing costume.)

But you don't have to spend thousands of dollars on a vacation at the beach (although a trip there, if you forget about the indignities of the airports and the flights, can certainly be a fabulous—and definitely relaxing—experience) in order to be able to take it easy and detox yourself from everyday stress. One of the first things I teach my students is that it's perfectly all right and safe to relax. That's the biggie. Our entire lives are now nothing but stress. We go to sleep with stress and wake up with stress. And the more hectic the city or place where you live, inevitably the more stressful your life will be.

Super Callanetics can counteract all of that. Every time you do Super Callanetics, you're actually teaching yourself how to relax. It's why you'll hear me saying, *Relax your body*, over and over, during the different exercises. I can never say it enough, and you can never be too relaxed while doing Super Callanetics. As many of my students have told me, Super Callanetics really is a fabulous substitute for a tranquilizer. And so much healthier! Thousands of people have been able to stop taking diuretics and laxatives, tranquilizers and other drugs, because Super Callanetics has improved the overall state of their bodies so much that they've no longer needed any synthetic help for problems they thought would never go away. And if you're exhausted, or worn-out, or angry, or just plain frazzled, Super Callanetics is better than any drug—because it's your body working for you.

Not only that, but as you learn to control your muscles, it's impossible not to begin to truly appreciate just how wonderful a creation your body is. Every muscle in your body is meant to be used. Your muscles are there for a *reason*. And when those muscles are used, they strengthen all the other parts of your body, including your bones. I recently had a physical, and I thought the doctor would tell me I was shrinking. Instead, I was completely shocked when I was told that I, at fifty-one years of age, measured a half inch taller than I had ever been! I thought there had to be a silly blunder, and I made him measure me again and again. It was no mistake. I was actually half an inch taller, and this is at an age (and with my history of back and bone problems) when I thought I'd be shrinking! Doing Super Callanetics is like getting a healthy shot of preventive medicine. I attribute my 'growth' to all the wonderful stretching of my spine, as well as the strengthening of the muscles that support my skeleton. I no longer slump over. It's almost like having a guarantee that you'll be standing, erect and firm, when you're eighty years old.

The Difference Between the One-Hour Callanetics Program and Super Callanetics

Do you remember how you felt after your very first hour of Callanetics? You felt an incredible internal sensation— and a wonderful awareness that your muscles had been working. Many people have remarked to me that they didn't know exactly *what* that feeling was— only that it felt *amazing*. That's how you feel when your muscles are getting stronger. With Callanetics, you can build up an *incredible* amount of muscle strength after only one hour, and as you continue stretching your spine and strengthening your muscles, you keep getting stronger and more flexible. Your body is becoming tighter and more beautiful, and that means you're doing Callanetics the right way.

Super Callanetics will allow you to feel this even more. Learning to do these intense exercises is a revitalizing experience. It's also an excellent challenge.

The basic difference between the one-hour program and Super Callanetics is simple. Each motion of Super Callanetics is basically the equivalent of *twenty* of the one-hour movements. So the results are *twenty* times as effective and noticeable.

The minute you do Super Callanetics, you will feel just how much deeper these exercises work, for faster results.

If you have already seen the Super Callanetics video, you'll know that I often say, Curl your pelvis up more than you think you can. Staying curled up helps deepen the contractions of the specific muscles you're working, and helps your body perform quite efficiently.

I also realized when I began teaching Super Callanetics that if you are curled up more, the little motion you need to do when you are curled up becomes even smaller. Being able to control your muscles in such a short range of motion requires a great deal of strength, and helps explain why Super Callanetics is so effective at tightening up your body faster—and keeping it tight. The better and more advanced your position, the less you will be able to move. That is how it should be.

19

By now, you will have noticed that some of the movement in the exercises seems almost imperceptible. Well, you're not wrong in thinking that. Many of the Super Callanetics exercises use only one-sixteenth to one-quarter of an inch of motion. Take out a ruler and see just how tiny one-sixteenth of an inch really is. It's *minuscule*!

You may also remember, if you have seen the video, that I often tell you to move one-half inch, not one-sixteenth to one-quarter inch. This is because so many people have written to say that after they have become stronger, they find that they are easily able to move *less* than one-half inch. So you can start off by gently moving one-half inch for all of the exercises. When you feel that you have comfortably mastered them, gradually work up to one-quarter inch. Your ultimate goal is to move no more than one-sixteenth inch. Look at your ruler again. It certainly *is* a challenging goal.

Remember, in Super Callanetics, *Less is more*.

And don't be deceived by these little movements. They are incredibly powerful!

When You Are Ready to Begin Super Callanetics

Please: You must read the section A Few Tips Before You Begin on pp. 33 before you start doing any Super Callanetics exercises.

Before *ever* attempting any of the Super Callanetics exercises, you must be completely familiar with all the movements, terms, and exercises from the one-hour program, and have built up strength from doing them regularly. I cannot stress this enough. Even Mike Tyson couldn't begin to attempt Super Callanetics without having mastered the entire one-hour program, even though we all know how 'strong' he is. You need *at least* ten to fifteen hours, depending on the individual, of solid experience with the one-hour program before ever attempting Super Callanetics.

Many of my students are very surprised when I tell them that I have already taken them—unknowingly—into some of the Super Callanetics movements *if* I have seen that they have the proper muscle strength for them. It all depends on the individual. Some people find the Buttocks exercises very difficult during their first few hours in Callanetics, and the Stomach exercises very easy (or vice versa). If you find that's true for you, you might want to gradually incorporate some of the Super Callanetics exercises in your regular Callanetics exercise program, while still remaining in the one-hour program for all the other exercises. When you have comfortably improved in other areas, then move on to Super Callanetics.

Other people are never able to stretch as much as they like, because flexibility is really based on genetics (and their genes pooped out in the stretching arena!). You can either do splits and try out for the cheerleading squad, or wonder just how those girls can extend their legs so easily when you can barely lift yours off the floor! (To say nothing of those glorious chaps on the gymnastics teams.) There are also other factors involved—how flexible you were when you were younger, and how quickly you might be able to regain some of the flexibility; how stiff you might be after a hard day sitting at your desk at work; and how tired you might be that morning, for example. Of course, some other people possess a terrific stretching ability and don't even know it . . . because

they've never attempted it! But most body types do have the ability to improve their flexibility to a greater extent.

What *you* can do is make the most of *your own potential*.

It doesn't matter what shape you're in—stretching is as important as brushing your teeth. What you should *never* do is torture yourself if you find stretching to be difficult. You cannot expect miracles when you first start. If you aren't very flexible, you must keep at it at *your* level, or chances are you could have problems and injuries later in life. Be patient. Never force yourself into a position that might feel uncomfortable. Do not compare yourself to anyone else who may be stretching in the room with you—what is a tremendous and successful stretch for that person might not be the same for you. (For this reason, you should never stretch with another person. He or she will not know your stretching abilities on that specific day, and can pull you just a tad too much—and this can create an injury.) Even some ballet dancers, who have been training their bodies since they were children, do not have and will *never* have the ability to fully stretch and extend themselves as much as they would like to. That knowledge does not keep them from stretching every day. They know—and *you* should know by now—that one should only do as much as one can, gently, and listen to one's body. If you start to feel any strain, ease up on either the stretch or the exercise. Cut back on your repetitions. Modify your Super Callanetics program for the particular day. And if ever your body says stop, *Stop!*

How Often Should I Do Super Callanetics?

You certainly don't have to do Super Callanetics every day! Since Super Callanetics is so much more powerful and effective than the one-hour program, some of you—if you do all these exercises correctly, with your heart and soul—will find that you may only have to do it once a week. One hour of Super Callanetics per week is much more than the equivalent of two one-hour Callanetics sessions.

Or you may wish to alternate between one one-hour Callanetics and one Super session each week. And because there are more exercises in Super Callanetics, you can pick and choose from the exercises you like and do the best and create your own individualized Callanetics exercise program.

Others will find that two sessions of Super Callanetics are necessary to maintain that lovely tight body. However many sessions of Callanetics you are accustomed to doing, Super Callanetics should halve that number.

Once you become even stronger, you can gradually increase the reps of some of the exercises, for more of a challenge. Doing so will not take any longer than a few extra minutes.

Don't forget that if, for instance, you find yourself with an unusually heavy workload one week and unable to do a full session of Super Callanetics, you have other choices. You can try the Twenty-Minute Program on page 155, or it's quite simple to incorporate some of the exercises into your daily routine. Stuck in line at the supermarket or waiting for the lift? Try some of the standing Buttocks—Outer Thighs—Hips exercises, such as Out to the Side. Or perhaps you need a pick-me-up in the office and the doughnut-and-tea cart is rolling by. Stand up and do a few Underarm Tighteners or Neck Relaxers—or even an Up and Down if you have the room—and see how your vitality returns in an instant. Super Callanetics is certainly a lot better for your figure than a jelly doughnut!

And what is most important . . . is to have fun with Super Callanetics. Be creative. You are doing Super Callanetics for you. It's your body, and you know how well it can work, at its own speed. Every time you make that little motion, moving only one-sixteenth to one-quarter inch, you are gently tightening and shaping your body even more.

How Super Callanetics Can Help You

Using Super Callanetics as a Warm-up

Athletes are often surprised when they find out that Super Callanetics is one of the best warm-ups there is before their intense workouts. Anything you do that raises your body temperature is, really, a warm-up. Your body needs to be warmed up before strenuous sports activity or it is very likely that injuries will result to muscles, tendons, and ligaments. They need a chance to warm up and become more pliable before being vigorously stretched. And your body also needs to be stretched *after* exercising to counteract all the work your muscles have been doing. Stretching itself is not a warm-up! If you try to stretch when your muscles are 'cold,' you can really hurt yourself.

With Super Callanetics, your muscles will be working extremely deeply without your worrying about how warm they are. Super Callanetics *is* a warm-up! You don't need to do the entire Super Callanetics program as your warm-up. Choose which section works best for your particular sport or art.

And people who do Super Callanetics properly don't get injuries. Why? Because your muscles will work *only* when they are ready—not when you command them.

How Super Callanetics Can Improve Your Performances

SKIERS

Professional skier Albert Bianchine lives and teaches skiing in Vail, Colorado, and he discovered Callanetics when he was browsing in a bookstore two years ago. 'When I was going through the Callanetics book, I quickly saw that these were very good exercises, and as soon as I started skiing, I noticed a tremendous difference in my abilities—my mobility, endurance, and flexibility all improved a great deal. And my inner thighs would never get as tired.

'There's a tremendous problem with skiers in the West,' he continues, 'which is that people arrive here from all different elevations, which is quite taxing on the body. Not only is skiing incredibly demanding physically, especially when armchair athletes are not in particularly good shape when the season starts, but they suffer the additional altitude stress here when they hit the slopes. This leads to all sorts of injuries, especially if people aren't properly warmed up.

'This is why Callanetics has helped me, and other skiers, so much. I knew that some skiers were skeptical about how Callanetics works, since it's not aerobic exercising, but when I looked at the program, I was basically more curious than skeptical. I also knew Callanetics was soundly designed. I was also lucky that Callan herself came to Colorado for workshops, and I learned from her. Now, I consider myself to be in excellent shape, but she put me through a workout that had me very surprised about my own athletic strength. Boy, was I fooled! Doing Callanetics is an incredible experience.

'What I'd also like to say is how much Callanetics has helped my lower back. Skiing, especially when you hit the moguls, always stresses your lower back. I suddenly realized that I could ski all week with no pain—Callanetics has helped relieve much of the stress and tension on my lower back.

'I only wish that Callan would move out here! Hopefully a Callanetics franchise will open here soon, so that other skiers can benefit from all the exercises that have helped me so much.

'I am ready for Super Callanetics.'

SINGERS

Ann Whitney is a professional opera and musical-comedy singer, and when she began doing Callanetics, she found some surprising results. 'When you sing, you especially use your diaphragm, stomach and back muscles,' she explains. 'I found that Callanetics had strengthened these muscles so much that I could expand my rib cage much more to take bigger breaths, and I could hold my tones and phrases much longer as well.

'I also felt a lot more confident about my body', she adds. 'It got much stronger, and this helped free up my breathing. I feel like the notes are just flowing right out, instead of sounding tight and constricted.'

Another benefit of Super Callanetics is how it helps your posture, which is especially important for performers who might be onstage for hours. 'When you sing you need to be "grounded,"' Ann explains. 'If you start slouching, your whole chest can cave in. You not only have no room to breathe properly, but you sound terrible! Callanetics and Super Callanetics have taught me how to open myself up and stand comfortably. I now know that all the muscle strength I need is there, to expand and work for *me*. I also know that I control my body, rather than its controlling me. Now I never have to worry about how I'm standing or what I'm doing when I'm singing. All I have to do is sing!'

BALLET (AND OTHER) DANCERS

Cindy Bennett is a professional ballerina, and she also found some very interesting results when she began doing Callanetics. 'I used to think I knew everything and was really strong,' she says, laughing at herself. 'Doing Callanetics was really quite the humbling experience.

'You see,' she continues, 'I didn't think the exercises would be difficult at all for me to do because I have been trained to be in perfect control of my body. And dancers have to be especially aware of everything going on with their bodies, because that's our *life*!

'But when I started doing Callanetics, I actually could not do the Hip and Buttocks exercises. You'd think they would be the easiest ones of all for a trained dancer. I was *so* embarrassed!'

She stuck with it, however, and soon found—much to her surprise—that her

25

buttocks, which had been as tight as they could be from years of dancing and stretching, actually became even tighter. Their entire shape changed . . . for the better, of course!

'Callanetics not only shaped my buttocks, but it helped the muscles a ballet dancer uses to "turn out" into position,' Cindy adds. 'And because my legs became so much stronger, I found I could leap higher. My work *en pointe*—in toe shoes—became better and more precise. And all the stretching at the end improved my leg extensions—how high my legs can go.'

Other dancers have had similar results. But as you already know, you don't have to be a professional *anything* to use and enjoy the benefits of Callanetics.

Cindy is ready for Super Callanetics.

How Super Callanetics Can Help Your Posture

When I first left home to conquer the world (don't you love the arrogance of youth?), I ended up traveling for over a decade. Because I lived in so many foreign countries, I intentionally learned the manners and customs of each country where I stayed in order not to offend any of the local inhabitants. These usually were countries where the male was 'the god' and the female was 'the mule' (and often 'the plow' as well). Continuing on my innocent merry way from country to country, I didn't realize how instinctively I had changed my posture to take on the submissive appearance of the female and remain unobtrusive.

Japan was the straw that broke the camel's back. There, I was always bending over in order not to draw attention to myself (which only served to aggravate my bad back condition even more), placing my hand in front of my mouth before and after speaking, and holding my head down when I would be talking to men which is the custom for women there. But when I arrived back in the United States, I found that the appearance I gave to Westerners was that of a pathetic wimp, and that I had become the unwitting yet perfect target for bullies.

One of the things that changed my wimpiness through the eyes of the Westerner was, obviously, my posture. The more I did the program, the more erect I stood and walked . . . the more self-confidence I had, the more people accepted me as their equal. As I moved on to Super Callanetics, my posture became even more erect, and my confidence became so much stronger that whenever I entered a room filled with people, almost everyone would stare at me, wondering who I was. Again, through their eyes, I had become more than their equal. It wasn't so much that it was me—it was their perception of who I was because of my *posture*.

The way you hold yourself is sending messages to the world, whether positive or negative. Imagine walking into a room with the CEO and all the board members of an excruciatingly important company waiting to interview you for the job of your lifetime, representing their firm. First impressions are always the most important. You will never get this coveted job—or any other of consequence—if you walk in slumped over, your stomach protruding, your buttocks sticking out, and your head hanging.

And posture can give away so many of your inner feelings. Why do you think the muggers in the street know whom to mug? They judge their victims by their energy and posture. As horrible as that is—it's their profession.

Super Callanetics has freed me from worries about my posture. What is so amazing for me is that I remembered how I had been taught as a child to walk with a book on my head. I had forgotten these silly but all-important childhood lessons, and paid a very high price for becoming unaware of how my body looked to the rest of the world. Thanks to Super Callanetics, I can now enter any room, head high, body erect yet relaxed, and know that no one will ever think I am a subservient female again!

How to Do Super Callanetics

I've heard every excuse in the book not to begin Callanetics and Super Callanetics! People say they're too old . . . it's too late . . . they're fat because it's 'hereditary' . . . they know Super Callanetics can't work for them. My favorite is the 'thyroid problem.' These people are convinced that all their weight and body problems stem from underactive thyroids. For a very very small percentage of people, that may be true—but if you do think your inability to lose weight is caused by a medical prob-

27

lem, you *must* see a doctor immediately.

Others try one session and never return. They want to look good, but aren't willing to commit themselves and do what they have to do for a beautiful body. Instead, they spend all their time complaining about how dreadful their bodies look and make them feel.

They don't know what they're missing!

You don't need any special clothing, special props, or special preparation to do Super Callanetics. You can do Super Callanetics whenever and wherever you want . . . in the morning, afternoon, or evening. In a special exercise room with a barre, or on a mat in your bedroom, even watching your favorite television program, using a piece of living-room furniture for balance. In the backyard, or even in the dark, if that's what you prefer! All you need is an hour of uninterrupted time (although, I must confess, sometimes I do talk on the phone when I'm doing Super Callanetics— as long as it's a *cordless* phone!).

About the Barre

You will notice that many of the exercises in Super Callanetics are done at the barre.

As you know from *Callanetics*, *Callanetics for Your Back*, or *Callanetics Countdown*, sturdy furniture can always be substituted for any of the barre exercises.

Do, however, use a padded exercise mat or folded towel for any floor exercises that involve kneeling, so that you can protect your knees from accidental bruising. You may also want to keep a suction-cup type of bath mat handy, to place under your feet in case you feel like you are about to slip during any of the standing exercises.

And don't forget that you should *never* use a towel rack to support your weight during the Open and Close exercise. They aren't designed for anything other than towels!

About Hanging

If you have already browsed through this book or have seen the Super Callanetics video, you may have noticed that one of my favorite warm-ups and spine stretches—the Hang—is nowhere to be found. There is a very good reason for this. I have found that too many people were 'hanging themselves' irresponsibly. One woman wrote to tell me she was hanging from a sapling branch—and it broke! Well, what did she expect?

I absolutely adore hanging. It stretches the spine so beautifully. But most people do not have access to the type of high ladder barre I have in my exercise studio, and they find it uncomfortable to hang from a door (as I suggested in the *Callanetics* book).

If you are determined to hang, please make a small investment in a durable chinning bar, and install it properly. Then you can hang from it to your heart's content. Start with a hang that lasts no longer than a count of three. As you build up the strength in your wrists, gradually work up to about a count of sixty. Never, as you know by now, hang longer than is comfortable. Your body should always remain perfectly relaxed.

What Not to Wear

SHOES

As you will have noticed from my other books and videos, I never wear anything on my feet other than ballet slippers. (Actually, I prefer to go barefoot, but my feet get a wee bit too dirty during a photo session for me to show them to you. Eagle-eyed viewers will notice, however, that I am barefoot in several of the photographs in this book!) Feel free to wear ballet slippers, socks, or just be barefoot—whatever you prefer. (If you are exercising on a slippery floor, be sure to keep a suction-cup–type bath mat nearby to place under your feet should you find yourself losing your balance.)

Shoes are simply too heavy to wear during any Super Callanetics exercises. If you tried wearing aerobics shoes during the Buttocks exercises, they'd end up feeling like five hundred-pound weights after only a few reps! They can also throw you off balance.

If, however, your physician has prescribed orthotics for you, and you are accustomed to wearing them in your workout shoes, please feel free to continue wearing them, but only for the standing exercises.

TIGHTS

The only thing I insist upon when I am teaching is that my students *do not* wear tights that act as a girdle, unless your doctor recommends them. They can affect your circulation. The only girdle you should be wearing is that of your own muscles! That's the best and the most natural.

And then there is the problem of pulling these 'tight' tights on and pulling these 'tight' tights off—this can aggravate preexisting back problems (as well as ruin a perfectly good manicure!).

And frankly, my experience has been that using clothes to disguise your true shape is not good for you during a Super Callanetics session. Then you will always think that your body looks better than it actually does. If you can't see your body or feel what your muscles are doing, you won't work as hard.

Mirrors

Before you get carried away admiring your new Super Callanetics–shaped body, however, I do need to say something about all those mirrors you might find yourself staring in. Although mirrors are extremely useful for you to be able to see your positions during many of the Super Callanetics exercises, it is very important that you not become *obsessed* with them. You should be able to *feel* your body

working for you. Your muscles respond to what you tell them to do. You *don't* need a mirror if you *feel* the exercises properly. Remember what happened to Narcissus!

About Music

You may recall that I also have fairly strong feelings about music. When you first began the one-hour program, I advised that no music be played. For one thing, it's almost impossible not to try and keep up with the beat when you hear it; moving to rhythm is instinctive. (That's great if you're out dancing, but not when you're doing Callanetics and Super Callanetics!)

For another, many people who have done aerobic dance–type exercise have become accustomed to hard, pushy music. Even when I tried exercising to loud music, I felt great immediately afterward, but not long after that I would suddenly find myself completely wiped out, instead of having energy that would last for days.

Well, since you already know that my philosophy is the total opposite of almost everything that's out there in the universe, I must confess that all the screaming and hollering and thrusting that goes on in some exercise classes is enough to have most people carried off to the loony bin (if only for a rest).

So I've found that exercising to either no music, or very soothing sounds such as those you'll hear on the Super Callanetics video, is much more conducive to a relaxing session. It's like going to a house of worship or spending time alone with your Creator: many people like to go even though they're not particularly religious, because it's so peaceful and calm. It gives them a little chance to get away from all the noise out there. And noise bombards you, practically every second of the day. It hits your nervous system and has a definite, negative effect. And I've found that the older you get, the more you need to find a haven of calm in which you can surround yourself. Loud music is great if you're eighteen, but most people as they grow older find that they prefer something that will soothe their souls and ease their spirits (and not make their ears ring for hours).

Instead, use the time you spend doing Super Callanetics to cleanse your mind of all negativity. Feel that your body is so

light you could soar and glide in the air like a bird—but not a hummingbird. You can get exhausted watching those precious little darlings flap their wings in triple fast motion!

I must add, however, that if you do prefer to do your Super Callanetics to punk rock or heavy metal or house music (or whatever else there is blaring on the radios all day long), don't despair (but do be careful not to damage your hearing). Once you've mastered Super Callanetics, you will possess such tremendous control of your muscles that you will be able to exercise to any kind of music you want—for you will have trained your mind and body to respond only to the delicate, tiny, controlled motions. Music will have no effect on how you perform Super Callanetics—other than to please your ears.

About Breathing

When I first started teaching, some of my students were so used to 'heavy breathing' that it often got out of hand in class! People were so deeply involved in their breathing technique that they would forget how to do the exercises! It would also become very disturbing to the other students, who were relaxed and calm—all of a sudden they would hear this great big *whooosh!* of an inhale, and then this great big *whooosh!* of an exhale, usually followed by some rather revolting slobber! I'd even see people sitting and taking their pulse during class. How conditioned we humans can become.

And so I kept thinking . . . something is not quite right. Here are all these people whose hearts, supposedly, are in top-notch condition—but their bodies: yuck! Just *unbelievably* unpleasant to look at, especially the gooshy hanging skin.

When you're doing Super Callanetics, just remember to breathe *naturally,* and you won't have any problems.

The Key Words

There are certain words and phrases I love, and by now you should know them all by heart. Yet these are the keys to what makes Super Callanetics so effective for you. So here they are—again!

❏ *Always work at your own pace*

❏ *Listen to your body*
❏ *Never, ever force*
❏ *Gentle, delicate little motions*
❏ *Light as a feather*
❏ *Flowing like a feather*
❏ *Relax your entire body*
❏ *Your body is like a rag doll*
❏ *Let yourself drip into the floor*
❏ *Never compare yourself with anybody else*
❏ *Triple slow motion*

Using the Key Words to Do Super Callanetics at Your Own Speed

All of us are different. Thank goodness for that! And all of our bodies are shaped and sized very differently as well. Which is why I have always stressed that you should *never compare yourself with anybody else.* Super Callanetics is not a race. The clock is not ticking. No one is timing you, or expecting you to reach the finish line with everyone else. It doesn't matter how many reps anybody else has counted. You can only compare yourself with what you are capable of doing. So, always remember to *work at your own pace.*

Most important, *listen to your body.*

And *never, ever force.*

One of my favorite words is *gentle.* It's a kind, kind word, and it even sounds sweet. When you are gentle with your body, you are showing it the respect it deserves. If you don't, it's like putting fine bone china in the dishwasher (and that's asking for trouble!). All of your movements in Super Callanetics must be gentle. Flowing, and delicate. *As light and flowing as a feather.*

Relax your entire body.

Listen to your body.

Always work at your own pace.

A Few Tips Before You Begin

Some of the terms I have been using ever since I developed the first Callanetics program can easily be misinterpreted by those of you who are unfamiliar with my exercise vocabulary. Please read this section before you begin any Super Callanetics session.

REPS

A 'rep' is simply an abbreviation for 'repetition.' This means how many times you should repeat an exercise.

REPEAT TO OTHER SIDE

Super Callanetics exercises always begin on the right side. If, for example, you are doing your exercises for the buttocks, you will be sitting on your left side, but you will be *working* your *right* side. Nearly every exercise is repeated on the other side.

COME OUT OF POSITION

After you have finished doing your exercise, relax, and, in triple slow motion (see page 35), come out of whatever position you were working in. Instructions on how to come out of each position are provided at the end of each exercise.

TAKE A BREATHER

People have written me, saying that they thought 'taking a breather' meant they could get up, go to the kitchen, have a cup of tea, talk on the phone with a friend, and then resume Super Callanetics whenever they felt like it. *It doesn't* (although I must say I like the idea)! At that pace, it would take you three days to do a one-hour program if you 'took a breather' every time this book says 'take a breather'!

What 'take a breather' really means is a little bit different. If you find that the exercise you are doing is becoming difficult, *take a breather*. Take yourself out of whatever position you are in, breathe deeply for a few seconds, just relax, and then resume the correct position.

And remember to keep breathing naturally throughout all of the exercises.

Never hold your breath!

WORK AT YOUR OWN PACE

Each and every day is a different one, and your body responds differently to exercise as well, for many reasons. On some days, you will be loose and limber, and exercising will seem a breeze. You'll be able to do one hundred reps without a second thought. But the next day, you might only be able to do twenty, and start to panic. It may be simply that the weather is lousy or your car might have broken down or you ate something that is just lying there in your stomach or work is incredibly taxing and you're so stressed-out that you don't know which way to turn. Or your muscles may simply be tired. *Don't worry!*

Relax. Respect your body. Take it easy.

Do a lighter session than usual, with fewer reps of exercises that might seem particularly difficult. If you are really having a tough time, perhaps you might want to stop for that day. Or you can go back to the one-hour program, and return to Super Callanetics for your next session.

Always listen to your body.

One of my favorite letters came from an eighty-year-old man in Arizona. He wrote to tell me that he couldn't wait to go to bed at night, because he knew that when he woke up, he would be doing Super Callanetics. Whenever I'm having a bad day, I think of him, and instantly feel inspired. I am certain that this man always listens to *his* body! If he didn't, he could never do Super Callanetics!

HIP-WIDTH APART

Stand up, and place your hands on your hipbones. Now look down at your feet. They should be lined up with your hips. This gives you better balance. For most people, hip-width is about a foot apart. Try placing a ruler between your feet so you have a perfect idea of what twelve inches looks like!

CURL YOUR PELVIS UP

By now, you should be able to curl your pelvis up in your sleep! This movement, as you know, is so crucial to all Callanetics and Super Callanetics that I am repeating how to do it.

I still find that when I'm teaching, I need a lot of patience working with new students on the pelvis. Many—both men and women—don't even know where it is, much less what to do with it. (No wonder there are so many divorces!) And then when they do find it, learning how to move it flowingly makes them feel incredibly exposed and vulnerable. It can be an excruciatingly self-conscious area for many people. And feeling that way is nothing to be ashamed about. Super Callanetics will help you dislodge your fears and self-consciousness about this area as it shapes and tones your body.

The pelvis, you see, is absolutely crucial for supporting your entire back. The pelvis is the key to your entire body posture. It affects how you sit, stand—how you *move*. The better you can move your joints in a smooth, fluid motion, the more you can stand tall and walk like a peacock. And being able to curl your pelvis up more than you think you can will contract your muscles even more. Curling your pelvis up is a terrific stretch for your lower back.

Remember: Tighten your buttocks. Curl your pelvis up and in toward your navel. Your back will automatically round.

You can always curl your pelvis up more than you think you can!

TRIPLE SLOW MOTION

By now, you should also be very familiar with this phrase! I know I've said it before, but I can never say it enough, and I think this is the best way to say it: All you are doing is watching a slow-motion sequence in a movie . . . slowing it down even more . . . and you are the star. Whatever move you make, you can slow it down even more . . . make it gentle . . . keep it flowing like a feather.

Special Note for All the Standing Exercises

At this advanced level, whenever you are instructed to stand with both feet on the floor, you may keep your legs straight but always have your knees relaxed—never locked.

35

WARM-UPS

Up and Down

THIS EXERCISE WILL HELP YOU STRETCH YOUR SPINE, AS WELL AS LOOSEN YOUR KNEES.

❏ Stand with your feet a hip-width apart. Stretch both your arms up to the ceiling as high as you can. Tighten your buttocks, and curl your pelvis up. Now stretch even more. Relax your knees—don't lock them—and keep your feet flat on the floor.

❏ In one smooth motion, gently bend your knees as much as you can, and lower your upper body towards the floor, with your arms reaching forward. It's as if you are trying to grasp an object on the floor in front of you. Your torso is stretching out and away.

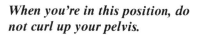

When you're in this position, do not curl up your pelvis.

❏ Gently swing your arms back, raising them as high as you can behind your body. Your knees will straighten slightly and your buttocks will raise with the motion of your arms going to the back and then up.

REMEMBER: *When you have swung your arms back, this will be one of the few instances where your pelvis will* not *be curled up.*

❏ Just as you're about to reverse the motion to go back up to your starting position, tighten your buttocks and curl your pelvis up even more than you think you can. Keep it curled up until you return, arms once again stretching up towards the ceiling.

5 TO 15 REPS

DOS AND DON'TS

❏ If you have a swayback, tip your pelvis up as much as you can.

❏ Do not arch your back while stretching your arms up to the ceiling.

❏ Totally relax your knees.

❏ Keep your shoulders relaxed.

❏ Let go of your neck.

❏ Your entire body is relaxed, including your feet.

The Swing

❏ This is basically the same gentle swinging stretch as Up and Down, except you will stay in a semicrouching position.

Your entire body is a rag doll.

❏ Just relax your knees. Relax your entire body. You are a rag doll sweeping your arms backward and forward as your knees gently move up and down.

❏ When you have finished, return to your standing position, vertebra by vertebra, remembering to tighten your buttocks and curl your pelvis up.

10 TO 15 REPS

DOS AND DON'TS

❏ Totally relax your knees.

❏ Keep your shoulders relaxed.

❏ Let go of your neck.

❏ Your entire body is relaxed, including your feet.

The Waist-Away Stretch

❑ Stand with your feet a hip-width apart. Put your left hand on your left hip, with your elbow out directly to the side. (Or, if it's more comfortable, place your hand on your thigh.) Reach your right arm up as high as you can. Bend your knees slightly.

Stretch over more than you think you can. Because of my congenital bone problems, I can't go over as far as I would like. Most of my students can go over to the side much further than I can, and straighten their extended arm more as well.

❑ Tighten your buttocks, and curl your pelvis up more than you think you can. Try to reach with your right arm even higher, until you feel your clothing moving up your right side. This will stretch your torso even more. Gently lean over to the left as far as you can, keeping your right arm straight, and then reach just a wee bit more.

❏ Move your torso up and down, not more than 1/16 to 1/4 inch, while stretching your right arm to the left in a smooth, continuous motion.

100 REPS

❏ To gently come out of this stretch, do not stand up straight. That would put pressure on your lower back. Instead, bend your knees as much as you can and gently stretch your right arm and torso, in front of you and then to your right, in one smooth, continuous motion. Feel your spine stretching.

Move over to the other side in one smooth, continuous motion.

❏ When you feel that your back is totally relaxed and that you can't go any further to the right, slowly come up to your original, starting position by tightening your buttocks, curling up your pelvis, and rounding up your torso, vertebra by vertebra.

❏ Repeat this exercise on the opposite side.

100 REPS

DOS AND DON'TS

- ❏ You can always stretch over more than you think you can.

- ❏ Relax your shoulders.

- ❏ Keep your outstretched arm as straight as you can, and as close to your head as possible.

- ❏ If you feel crunched on the opposite side you are stretching, you can always stretch that side of your body up even more.

- ❏ Relax your neck.

- ❏ Never bounce up and down; your movement during this stretch is almost imperceptible.

- ❏ Relax your knees.

Underarm Tightener

❏ Stand erect, feet a hip-width apart. Bend your knees a wee bit. Take your arms up and out to the side, keeping them perfectly straight and even with your shoulders. Slowly start rolling your hands forward so that your palms are face-up, thumbs aiming towards the ceiling.

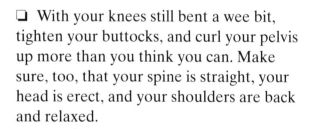

Even though you'll see that the legs are straight, the knees are relaxed.

❏ With your knees still bent a wee bit, tighten your buttocks, and curl your pelvis up more than you think you can. Make sure, too, that your spine is straight, your head is erect, and your shoulders are back and relaxed.

❏ Gently move your arms behind your back, trying to keep your hands even with your shoulders and your arms straight. Without jerking, move your arms 1/16 to 1/4 inch backward and forward.

100 REPS

❏ When you want to improve your balance while you're doing the back-and-forth motion, shift all your weight to one leg. Raise your other leg, bent, to where your ankle is at about knee height—or even higher (as you see in the photo here)—and stay in that position as long as it is comfortable.

50 REPS ON EACH LEG

The more control you have of your balance, the higher you can take up your knee.

ONCE YOU'VE MASTERED THAT BALANCE POSITION: *Try straightening your leg out, away from the body, as high as you can. Be sure, however, to keep your shoulders and hands even, your torso erect, and your raised leg relaxed.*

50 REPS ON EACH LEG

When you first attempt this balance position, you will probably want to bend your extended leg a little until you feel more confident with your weight on one leg.

❑ To come out of this exercise, gently, in triple slow motion, lower your leg to the floor. Then, delicately, bend your elbows and lower your arms.

REMEMBER: *The more erect your torso, the higher your arms are raised behind your body, and the more you can rotate your wrists, the more you will tighten your underarms, loosen the area between your shoulder blades, and stretch your chest muscles. Stretched chest muscles allow your shoulders to go back more. This is essential for correct posture.*

DOS AND DON'TS

❏ Keep your pelvis tipped up while both feet are on the floor.

❏ Gravity is always trying to pull your arms down, so keep them up as high as you possibly can.

❏ Relax your entire body, especially your neck.

❏ Don't lock your knees; keep them relaxed.

❏ When you are working on your balance, try to alternate standing on each leg for a count of 50.

Standing Hamstring Stretch

THIS STRETCH IS WHAT I ENJOY DOING WHEN MY LOWER BACK HAS BECOME STIFF AFTER SITTING FOR HOURS IN ONE POSITION.

(If you have mild sciatica, always keep your knees bent during this exercise, to relieve pressure on your sciatic nerve. If you have more than mild sciatica, avoid this stretch.)

❏ Stand erect with your feet a hip-width apart. Clasp your hands behind you, and gently try to raise your arms to the same level as if you were about to do the Underarm Tightener. Make sure your knees are relaxed.

❏ Very slowly, round your torso over, trying to touch your nose to your knees, or as far as you possibly can. Do not arch your back.

❏ If you are able to touch your nose to your knees, slowly continue to take your arms towards the floor as far as you can without forcing. If you are not quite that stretched, gently move your torso in triple slow motion, back and forth, 1/16 to 1/4 inch.

20 REPS, OR HOLD FOR A COUNT OF 20

REMEMBER: *Take advantage of this time to totally relax your neck. It should feel as if it is dripping into the floor.*

Even though the legs are straight, the knees are terribly relaxed—not locked.

48

❏ In one slow, smooth, and continuous motion, unclasp your hands and place them on the inside of each ankle. Your elbows are aimed out to the side, and your knees are still relaxed. If you need to move your feet apart another few inches for better balance, please do.

❏ Then slowly ease your head between your legs, as far as it will go, and move your torso back and forth, 1/16 to 1/4 inch.

20 REPS

❏ Gently move your torso over to your right side, clasping the outside of your right ankle with both hands. Bend your elbows out.

❏ Try to place your head in between your leg and your right elbow, and move your torso back and forth, 1/16 to 1/4 inch.

FOR MORE OF A STRETCH: *Bend both knees and move your left hip out to the side; this will shift some of your weight to that side. You should also feel this stretch in your lower back and buttocks muscles.*

FOR EVEN MORE OF A STRETCH: *Move your feet closer together. (You must have good balance for this position.)*

Keep your neck relaxed.

20 REPS

❏ Keeping your knees relaxed, gently move over to your left side, clasping the outside of your left ankle with both hands. Keep your elbows bent and out.

❏ Place your head in between your leg and your left elbow, and move back and forth, 1/16 to 1/4 inch.

FOR MORE OF A STRETCH: *Bend your knees even more, and shift your weight over to your right leg.*

20 REPS

❏ To come out of this stretch, very gently move your torso back to the center, in triple slow motion. With both legs relaxed, place your palms flat on the floor, if possible. If not, feel free to let your hands dangle wherever is most comfortable.

Your legs are bent and relaxed. Notice how rounded the body still is.

❏ Bend your knees as much as you possibly can, bringing your buttocks down so you are in a crouching position, with your hands still flat on the floor, or wherever is most comfortable.

❏ Tighten your buttocks, curl your pelvis up, and slowly round your torso up one vertebra at a time. Your arms should be hanging straight, loose and relaxed.

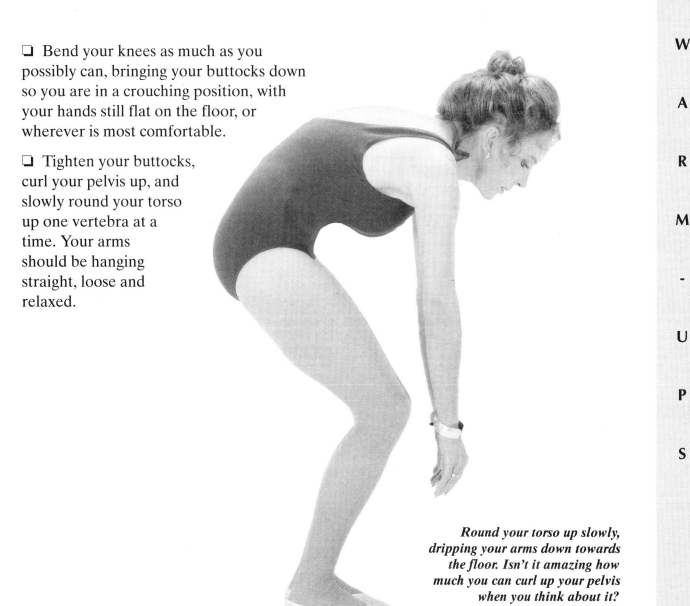

Round your torso up slowly, dripping your arms down towards the floor. Isn't it amazing how much you can curl up your pelvis when you think about it?

DOS AND DON'TS

❏ Do not tighten or lock your knees.

❏ Keep your hips even.

❏ Keep your entire back relaxed.

❏ Keep your movements fluid and small. Do not ever make hard, jerky movements.

❏ Relax your neck.

Neck Relaxer #1

❏ Stand erect, feet a hip-width apart. Your body is totally relaxed. Pretend your shoulders are melting to the floor. Tighten your buttocks, and curl your pelvis up more than you think you can.

❏ In triple slow motion, roll your head down, resting your chin on your chest.

Always keep your shoulders down and relaxed when you are doing these Neck Relaxers.

❏ Still slowly, move your chin over to your right shoulder as far as you can.

❏ Then aim your chin up towards the ceiling, as high as you can, at the same time stretching the back of your neck. You can stretch your neck more than you thought possible.

❏ Next, stretch your neck up even more than you thought possible.

❏ Delicately bring your chin back down to your chest.

❏ Gently move your chin over your left shoulder, and then stretch it up as high as it will go.

❏ Bring it back down to where your chin touches your chest again.

5 COMPLETE HALF-CIRCLES TO EACH SIDE

Neck Relaxer #2

❏ In the same stance, with your body relaxed, shoulders melting into the floor, buttocks tightened, pelvis curled up, and knees relaxed, gently look over to your right side as if you were having a conversation with someone standing in back of you, and hold for a count of 5.

❏ In triple slow motion, turn your head to where you are looking over your left shoulder, and hold for a count of 5.

❏ When you are finished, move your head back to center.

Always move in triple slow motion and think beautiful, soft thoughts.

5 REPS

DOS AND DON'TS

❏ Do not tense your shoulders; they must stay relaxed, dropping down to the floor. Don't let them move up—as they tend to do naturally if you're not thinking about it—when you are stretching your neck up.

❏ Do not move your body or your shoulders.

❏ Keep your buttocks tight and pelvis curled up.

❏ Keep your knees relaxed.

❏ Stretch your neck extremely gently when you move it.

STOMACH EXERCISES

Since you have already mastered Callanetics, you will be very familiar with the starting position for these exercises.

But please, it is absolutely crucial for you to remember that there are several very important differences between the stomach exercises in the one-hour Callanetics program and in Super Callanetics.

1. Starting Position

Before you even begin any of the stomach exercises, don't forget to have a towel or exercise mat handy, to place under your spine to protect it while you're on the floor.

I have noticed that many of my students become very nonchalant about the correct position for these exercises once they are familiar with how to do them. Yet rounding yourself up properly is so important! Do not get sloppy or lazy, because maintaining the lovely 'round' is what prevents you from putting pressure on your lower back, and too much force on your neck. The results are also much more noticeable!

REMEMBER: *When you are rounding up, your arms, neck, shoulders, and upper back flow as if they are one. Do not ever jerk your arms or neck to help you round up. Think gentle . . . think flowing . . . think* beautiful *round.*

2. How Much You Move

REMEMBER: *I've said that* Less *is more? Well, you will soon be noticing, if you haven't already, that many of the movements in Super Callanetics are actually* smaller *than those of the one-hour program. This is because it is actually* more *of a challenge to use a smaller range of motion—you have to have more control of your body to do this. (And because certain exercises require that you curl your pelvis up* even *more than you think you can, you will find that this actually* prevents *you from making a larger motion with your body.) Take out a ruler and measure 1/16 to 1/4 inch. It's barely even there! Even when you have mastered Super Callanetics, you must remember at all times to keep your movements tiny and almost imperceptible.*

3. Rounding Your Torso

In *Callanetics, Callanetics for Your Back*, and *Callanetics Countdown*, you will recall that your upper back was resting below your shoulder blades. Look at the photographs in this section, and you will immediately notice how rounded my shoulders are, and how far off the floor my upper back is. My stomach muscles are strong enough to maintain this position without straining the back.

Also bear in mind that the more you can grasp your legs and take your elbows out and up, the better the stretch of your upper back muscles. This, in turn, rounds your torso even more, allowing your stomach muscles to contract and work efficiently. The result is that you become stronger more quickly.

4. How to Get Up Off the Floor to Protect Your Back

One of the worst things you can do for your back is to jerk yourself up off the floor and just get up. It is very simple to learn how to get up gracefully, in a fluid, easy motion.

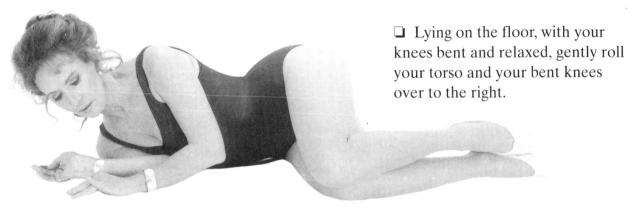

❏ Lying on the floor, with your knees bent and relaxed, gently roll your torso and your bent knees over to the right.

To begin getting up off the floor, roll onto your side.

Ease yourself up gently. This is no time for push-ups.

❏ Now place your hands on the floor over to your right side, and, in triple slow motion, ease yourself up to a sitting position.

❏ Then, using the strength of your arms, bring yourself up to a kneeling position. In triple slow motion, take your right leg up, bent, to where your right foot is resting on the floor.

Do not lock your elbows.

❏ Bring your left leg up. Tighten your behind and curl your pelvis up. Then gently, straightening up one vertebra at a time, return to a standing position.

Never *stand straight up after any Super Callanetics work—or* any *kind of work!—on the floor.*

Keep your back rounded. Roll yourself up, one vertebra at a time.

5. Don't Forget Your Neck

If your precious neck feels uncomfortable or hurts while doing any of the stomach exercises at the Super Callanetics level, this could be a sign that you may have a medical problem. Do not shrug off neck pain. It could be an indication that there is a long-standing problem, one that comes to your attention only after you begin doing certain kinds of body motions. For most people, this has turned out to be a blessing in disguise—because they went to their doctors and found out what was causing their problems. From there, they were directed to solutions.

Preventive medicine is like using plain old common sense. As I have said many times, *listen to your body*. Many people tend to ignore warning signals of potential problems—and then by the time they have to go to a doctor, it is often too late to correct a condition that could easily have been rectified earlier on.

Your body is the only one you have!

REMEMBER: *For all the stomach exercises where your body is resting on the floor, you can, if you prefer, put your hands behind your head, with your elbows out to the sides. In the advanced exercises, you will feel the stomach muscles working just as deeply.*

Bent-Knee Reach

❏ Lie on the floor, knees bent, feet flat a hip-width apart, and arms at your sides. Grab your inner thighs with all your might. Take your elbows out to the side as much as you can, and then aim them up towards the ceiling.

❏ Letting the small of your back be relaxed and melting into the floor, slowly round your head and shoulders up, off the floor. You will be rounding your nose into your chest. At the same time, bring your elbows out and up toward the ceiling even more. When you have rounded your torso as much as you possibly can, gently take your hands off your inner thighs and, keeping them inside your legs, grab the back of your legs higher to where you can round your torso and bring your elbows out and up even more.

Be certain to maintain that fabulous round! The elbows are out and up as far as they can go.

If your torso falls back a bit, don't worry; it's normal. Most people's stomach muscles are not strong enough to hold the advanced position, at first.

❑ Once your torso is rounded as much as possible, gently lower your arms, aiming them straight to the front of you, about 6 to 12 inches off the floor.

❑ Gently, in triple slow motion, do the tiny 1/16- to 1/4-inch motion, back and forth.

IF YOU FEEL THAT YOUR ENTIRE BODY IS MOVING BACK AND FORTH ON THE FLOOR: *Lift your feet 1 to 2 inches up off the floor. Moving back and forth or in a jerking motion is a signal that your back muscles are trying to come in to assist your stomach muscles.*

IF YOU FEEL THAT YOU ARE LOSING CONTROL OF THIS EXERCISE, OR THAT THERE IS A STRAIN ON YOUR LOWER BACK, EITHER: *Move your feet very slightly away from your body; or, take your torso down 1/16 inch. If it still feels too difficult, take your torso down another 1/16 inch.*

100 REPS

❑ To come out of this exercise, in triple slow motion, roll your torso down to the floor, one vertebra at a time.

REMEMBER: *Take your breathers when you have to. You may grab your inner thighs with your hands, as in the starting position, and hold your rounded position. Then, before releasing your hands to continue the exercise, take your elbows out and then up, and then round your torso even more. You may also roll down vertebra by vertebra to rest on the floor—but remember to start at Step 1 again when continuing with the exercises.*

Take a breather by holding on to the inside of the knees, elbows bent. I am still in the perfectly rounded position.

DOS AND DON'TS

❏ Do not tighten your stomach muscles. This puts pressure on your lower back. They will certainly be doing enough work!

❏ Just relax and let your lower back melt into the floor.

❏ Keep your torso and your shoulders rounded off the floor as much as possible.

❏ Do not move *just* your arms *or* your shoulders *or* your neck when pulsing. They all move with your upper torso as a unit.

❏ Relax your buttocks to take pressure off your lower back. They should not move at all.

❏ Relax your legs.

❏ Do not tense your neck.

❏ No jerking or bouncing.

REMEMBER: *When you are first getting into position, your nose should always be aimed into your chest. Once you have built up tremendous strength in your stomach muscles, you can either continue to keep aiming your nose towards your chest, or, you can raise your head just a tad, aiming your face towards your knees while doing your reps or taking a breather.* Never, *however,* aim *your face up towards the ceiling. You won't be changing the actual position of your neck—you only should be shifting the position of your head a wee bit. Do whatever is most comfortable for you.*

Single Leg Raise

Most people don't realize that they can actually point their toes without tensing their leg muscles. In the following exercises, as well as in the Leg section, whenever one or both legs are raised, point your toes, but remember to keep your legs perfectly relaxed. This is a wonderful opportunity to start training yourself to relax different parts of your body.

❏ Lying on the floor with your knees still bent, feet a hip-width apart, gently raise your right leg up, toes pointing towards the ceiling, grab the back of your thigh with both hands, below your knee. Both elbows are out as far as they can go, and then aiming up towards the ceiling.

❏ Now, in triple slow motion, round your torso up. At the same time, take your elbows out and then up even more to stretch the upper back. You are aiming your nose towards your rib cage.

❏ When you feel that you can't round any further, take your hands off your legs and extend them, straight out in the direction of your feet, 6 inches to 1 foot off the floor.

❏ Slowly straighten your left leg, raised no more than a foot off the floor.

❏ Now you are in position to gently move your torso, in triple slow motion, 1/16 to 1/4 inch, back and forth.

Relax your legs.

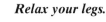

100 REPS

❏ When you feel comfortable with this movement, start to lower your upstretched leg 1/2 inch at a time. If you feel your lower back starting to take over—which is the signal that your stomach muscles are not quite strong enough —slowly raise your right leg back towards the ceiling, 1/2 inch at a time, until you feel no strain on your lower back.

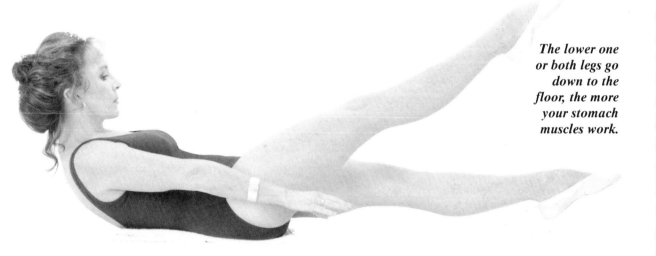

The lower one or both legs go down to the floor, the more your stomach muscles work.

IF YOU STILL FEEL PRESSURE ON YOUR LOWER BACK: *Either gently raise your upstretched leg towards the ceiling, or lower your torso 1/16 inch towards the floor, or rest your outstretched left leg on the floor.*

IF YOU NEED TO TAKE A BREATHER: *Bring your right leg up towards you, to where it feels comfortable, grasp it with both hands below your knee, hold your rounded-torso position with your elbows out, and breathe deeply and naturally. If you need to, rest your left leg on the floor or bend your left knee, resting your left foot on the floor.*

If your upstretched leg is low, bring it back up to a comfortable position for your breather.

When you are ready to start again, still holding on to your leg, round your torso more than you think you can, stretching your elbows out and up towards the ceiling. Let go of your leg, extend your arms out to your sides, then take your right leg down to the position it was in before your breather, and continue to count from wherever you left off. (Don't forget to extend your opposite leg off the floor if you have been resting it on the floor, or if it was bent.)

❏ To come out of this exercise, in triple slow motion—you have no choice!—gently bend your knees, one at a time, so that both feet are resting on the floor, and slowly lower your torso, vertebra by vertebra, until you are resting on the floor.

❏ Repeat this exercise on the opposite side.

100 REPS

DOS AND DON'TS

❏ Your entire body should be relaxed, like a rag doll.

❏ Do not let your back take over. Keep it relaxed. How much you can round your upper back depends on how stretched your upper back muscles are, and how strong your stomach muscles have become.

❏ If you feel the exercise is getting too difficult, or your back muscles are about to take over, raise your upstretched leg 1/2 inch higher. The lower you can take your raised legs down, the more your abdominal muscles will have to work—but they must be ready for such an *intense* workout.

❏ Keep your upper body rounded as much as you can.

❏ Keep your legs relaxed.

❏ Relax your stomach muscles.

❏ Relax your neck.

❏ Keep your elbows up and out as high as you possibly can, while getting into position.

❏ Do not ever aim your face towards the ceiling; this puts strain on your neck.

❏ Do not tighten your buttocks.

Double Leg Raise

❏ Lying on the floor, feet a hip-width apart, bend your knees up to your chest one at a time, and then extend both legs up towards the ceiling. Grab onto your outer thighs, stretch your elbows out then up as high as you can, then round your torso up with your nose pointing into your rib cage.

❏ Once you're rounded and in position, let go of your legs and extend your arms straight out, 6 inches to 1 foot off the floor.

As in the Single Leg Raise, lower your legs only as far as you can without feeling the strain in your lower back. Your legs should feel like feathers.

❏ In triple slow motion, lower your legs as far as is comfortable, then gently move your torso back and forth, 1/16 to 1/4 inch.

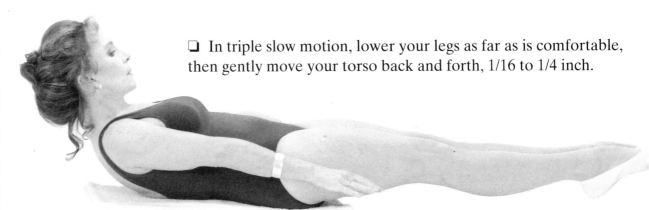

There should be no strain on your body at all—your lower back should always be on the floor, not arched. It takes incredible strength and control to lower your legs this much and still have your body feeling like a rag doll melting into the floor.

❏ If you feel that your lower back muscles are starting to take over, or your lower back is starting to arch, again, this is your signal that your stomach muscles are not yet strong enough to work at this level. Slowly raise your legs back up in 1/2-inch segments until you feel absolutely no pressure on your lower back, or your lower back does not arch, and then continue the exercise at that level.

100 REPS

IF YOU NEED TO TAKE A BREATHER: *Grab onto your outer thighs with both hands, hold your rounded torso position, with your elbows still aimed out to the side, and breathe deeply and naturally. Before letting go to continue the count, round your torso, and bring your elbows up and out more than you think you can.*

If your legs eventually go down as far as mine, for a breather, you will have to very gently bring them back up to a comfortable position so that you can easily hold onto your outer thighs.

❏ To come out of the double leg raise, in triple slow motion, bend your knees, and lower your feet to the floor, one at a time. Then lower your torso, vertebra by vertebra.

DOS AND DON'TS

❏ Your elbows must be out and up as far as they can possibly go for the starting position.

❏ Keep your shoulders rounded and up off the floor.

❏ Keep your entire body relaxed. Especially relax your legs and neck.

❏ Relax your stomach muscles.

❏ Do not let your lower back arch or come up off the floor. This is another signal that your stomach muscles are not quite strong enough to maintain that position. If so, bring your legs up 1/2 inch. If that's not enough, bring them up another 1/2 inch and continue until you have reached a comfortable position.

❏ Let your lower back melt into the floor.

❏ Relax your buttocks.

Sit Up and Curl Down

You will be working up to 4 sets of 10 reps each, lowering your torso only by curling up your pelvis. Each set becomes progressively more advanced. You must take a breather between each set.

For this exercise, 1 rep = 1 gentle wave of the arms up and down. Try to do 10 reps for each set.

❑ Sit up with your knees bent, feet a hip-width apart and flat on the floor, your hands clasped just below your knees. Put your head between your knees, with your elbows out to the side. Scoot your buttocks forward until you are not sitting on your tailbone.

When you scoot forward (first one buttock and then the other), it is similar to doing the pelvic curl-up, except you do not have to contract your buttocks muscles. Notice the position of the hands clasped below the knees.

❑ Tighten your buttocks and curl your pelvis up, which will automatically begin to lower your torso to the floor, vertebra by vertebra. Your back does not do any of the work, and does not move (other than being lowered by the action of your pelvis curling up). Very slowly, keep tightening your buttocks and curling your pelvis up until your curl-up lowers your torso enough so that your arms, which are still holding onto the side of your knees, are now straight. It usually takes 4 to 5 curl-ups to accomplish this.

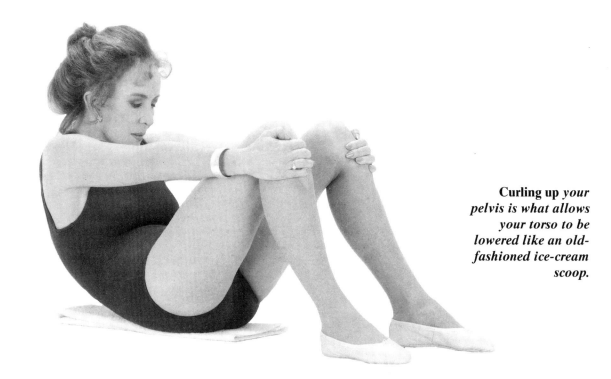

Curling up *your pelvis is what allows your torso to be lowered like an old-fashioned ice-cream scoop.*

❏ Without moving any other part of your body, let go of your knees. Your torso is still rounded and perfectly relaxed.

❏ With your arms straight, in triple slow motion, take them up as high as you can without forcing, and then back down to the floor in smooth, unbroken waves. Your body is balanced on the strength of your stomach muscles.

No other part of your body should be moving, except your arms, which will be flowing up and down.

10 REPS OF SLOW, GENTLE ARM WAVES FOR THIS FIRST SET

REMEMBER: *If you feel you are losing your balance, that is your signal that your stomach muscles are not yet strong enough to allow your arms to go as high as you are taking them. Don't take them up as high on the following reps. You can also slide your feet a few inches away from your body or round your torso more towards your knees (or do all three!).*

❏ Slowly clasp your hands up more towards the top of your knees and take a breather. Because your torso is lower now from curling your pelvis up you will need to clasp your hands higher on your knees. Hold your position, taking several deep breaths.

❏ When you are ready to continue, tighten your buttocks and curl your pelvis up even more. These curl-ups will take your torso even lower. Let go of your knees and begin your next set of slow, gentle arm waves.

Notice how much lower the torso is from the curl-up after taking a breather.

10 REPS FOR THIS SECOND SET

❑ To come out of your second set and begin your third set, grab the top of your knees, take a lovely breather, curl your pelvis up even more, take your hands off your knees . . . and continue your up-and-down waves with your arms.

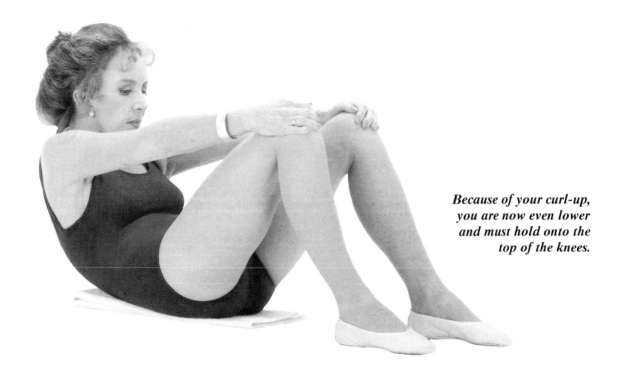

Because of your curl-up, you are now even lower and must hold onto the top of the knees.

10 REPS FOR YOUR THIRD SET

REMEMBER: *At this level, you will probably feel that you won't be able to take your arms up as high. Raise them only as high as is comfortable.*

❑ To come out of your third set and begin your fourth set without moving your body, put your hands above your knees (towards your thigh), take your breather, then continue the routine one more time.

10 REPS FOR YOUR FOURTH SET

❑ To come out of this exercise, slowly lower your torso—even if you are so low that you only have to go down a scant few inches—vertebra by vertebra, tipping your pelvis up more than you think you can as you ease back to the floor.

DOS AND DON'TS

❏ Keep your back as rounded as possible.

*This is the **wrong way** to do this exercise! If your back isn't rounded, this means you are balancing by putting pressure on your lower back, and **not** from the strength of your stomach muscles. Your back must remain rounded at all times.*

❏ Believe it or not, in a short time you will be able to curl your pelvis up so much more than you previously thought humanly possible!

❏ Try to bring your arms up as high as you can take them, without forcing. If this exercise is becoming too difficult, don't raise your arms higher than your ears. The more your torso has been lowered to the floor, the less high you will be able to raise up your arms.

❏ Concentrate on relaxing. Your arms, gently waving up and down, are the only part of your body that is moving at all.

❏ Keep your head down and neck relaxed.

❏ Breathe naturally.

❏ After each breather, curl your pelvis even more by rolling your pelvis in towards your navel.

❏ Do not jerk your pelvis.

Pelvic Ease-Down and Up

❏ Sit erect with your knees bent, feet a hip-width apart and flat on the floor. Scoot up your buttocks as in the previous exercise (Sit Up and Curl Down) so that you are *not* sitting on your tailbone.

❏ Place your head between your knees, and crisscross your hands at the base of your neck.

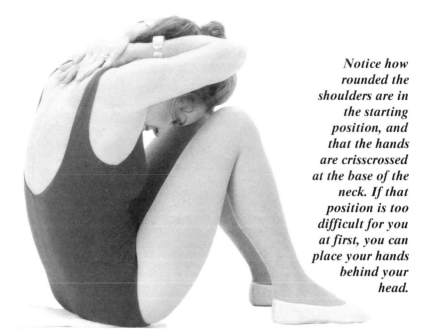

Notice how rounded the shoulders are in the starting position, and that the hands are crisscrossed at the base of the neck. If that position is too difficult for you at first, you can place your hands behind your head.

❏ Tighten your buttocks, and curl your pelvis up, which will automatically begin lowering your torso towards the floor. Keep your pelvis curled up—never releasing it—as you curl up. Your torso will lower with each curl-up, one vertebra at a time. In triple slow motion, ease yourself down, vertebra by vertebra, until you lie flat on your back. It should take 10 or more curl-ups to accomplish this.

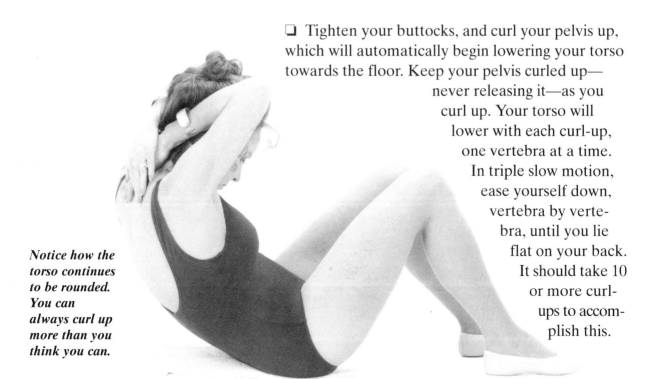

Notice how the torso continues to be rounded. You can always curl up more than you think you can.

❏ Rest on the floor for a few seconds, your arms still crisscrossed at the base of your neck.

REMEMBER: *Many people's stomach muscles will not be strong enough at this point to attempt to ease back up. This is much harder as you must now lift the weight of your torso against gravity to come up. And when you do attempt to ease back up, you will probably laugh—your muscles have to be lethal for you to accomplish this! Don't mentally beat yourself up if you can't do it yet—I don't think even Superman could do this one; it's so powerful! (Well, maybe he could if he didn't forget to wear his blue tights!) I must admit even I am shocked when I see men and women in their seventies coming back up with ease.*

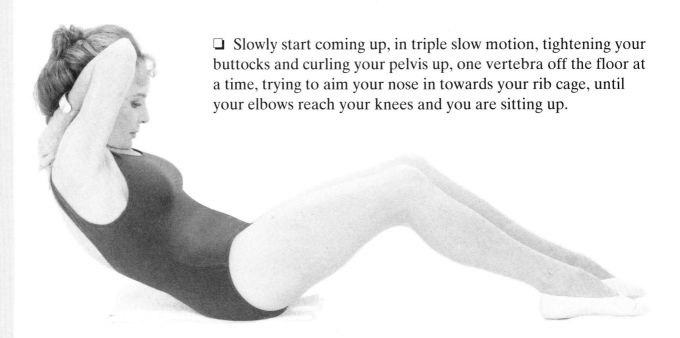

❏ Slowly start coming up, in triple slow motion, tightening your buttocks and curling your pelvis up, one vertebra off the floor at a time, trying to aim your nose in towards your rib cage, until your elbows reach your knees and you are sitting up.

Only attempt this reversal, curling slowly back up, if you are certain your stomach muscles are strong enough to support this position without your lower back taking over. At first, if you feel you are about to lose your balance, you will probably have to move your feet away from your body until your stomach muscles become extremely strong.

This is the total reverse of all the previous steps.

DO 1 REP DOWN AND IF YOU CAN, 1 REP UP, AT YOUR OWN PACE.

DOS AND DON'TS

❏ You must have incredibly strong stomach muscles to even attempt this exercise—but practice makes perfect.

❏ Keep your neck relaxed.

❏ You can always curl up more than you think you can.

❏ Only by tightening your buttocks and curling your pelvis up will you ease yourself down and up. Do not jerk or thrust your torso, or use your back to lower yourself down—or to bring yourself back up.

❏ Breathe normally.

❏ Relax your legs—they are like feathers.

Leg Exercises

Pelvic-Wave Leg Strengthener

In this exercise, you will be doing the pelvic wave, slowly down in three stages, and then back up.

By this time, you should be able to appreciate just how incredibly flexible and flowing the pelvis area can be. This is so necessary, as you know, for optimal health and posture.

Your legs should also be strong enough so that you won't ever find yourself holding onto your barre or piece of heavy furniture for dear life again!

One bit of advice, however: Do walk around for a few moments in between the Pelvic-Wave Leg Strengthener and the Plié and Balance exercises. This will give you a breather and help relax your muscles, enabling you to do these exercises more efficiently.

❑ Stand at your barre, or hold onto a piece of furniture, feet a hip-width apart, arms straight but relaxed. Go up on your *toes*—not the balls of your feet—knees bent, and bring your heels together, keeping your back straight and relaxed.

Notice how straight and relaxed the back is. And the knees are not forced out to the sides at all.

82

❏ In triple slow motion, with your torso erect and your neck stretched towards the ceiling, lower your torso 2 inches straight down towards the floor. Tighten your buttocks and curl your pelvis up. Then curl it up even more than you think you can, and at the same time allow your upper torso to round as much as possible. Hold for a slow count of 3, and then gently release your pelvis without pushing your buttocks back.

You can always curl your pelvis up more than you think you can.

❏ In triple slow motion, go down 2 more inches, tighten your buttocks, curl your pelvis up even more, hold for a slow count of 3, and gently release.

❏ Go down another 2 inches, tighten your buttocks, curl your pelvis up even more, hold for a slow count of 3, and gently release.

Feel how much your inner thighs are working at this level.

❏ Now reverse the movement, going up 2 inches each time, just as slowly, until you have returned to the original standing position. This equals 1 set.

DO 3 SETS

DOS AND DON'TS

❏ For the second and third sets, curl your pelvis up even more each time.

❏ Your spine is always straight when your pelvis is not curled up. Do not stick out your buttocks when coming out of the pelvic curl.

❏ Do not arch your back.

❏ Do not try to aim your knees out too far to the side. Let their position be natural.

❏ Keep your shoulders relaxed. Your upper back should be as rounded as possible when curling up the pelvis for the most beneficial spine stretch. The more your pelvis is curled up, the more your torso will round, stretching the spine, and the faster your legs will become strong and tight.

❏ Keep your balance on your toes.

❏ Do not lean your weight on the barre.

❏ When lowering your torso, do not allow your buttocks to go below your knees. This puts too much pressure on your knees.

Plié and Balance

❏ Beginning in the same position as the Pelvic-Wave Leg Strengthener, holding your barre or piece of furniture with both hands, your arms straight and loose, stand on your *toes* with your heels together.

❏ In triple slow motion, lower your torso straight down, 10 to 12 inches. Your torso is perfectly erect.

❏ In triple slow motion, raise yourself back up, breathing normally. This exercise is done in one smooth motion.

❏ If you wish, you can take your heels apart and balance even higher on your toes to make this exercise more difficult.

20 REPS

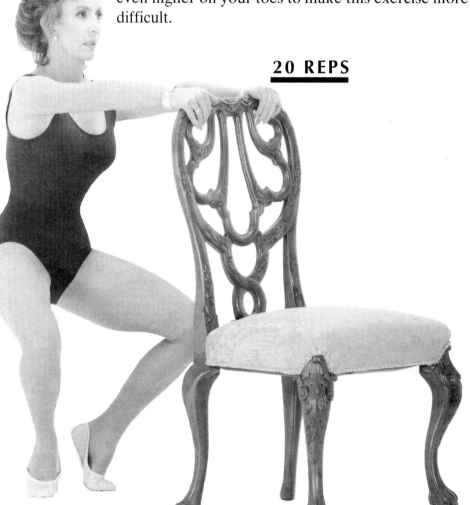

Even though the heels are apart and I am balancing up even higher on the toes, my back is perfectly straight!

IF YOU WANT A MORE INTENSE EXERCISE: *Hold your lowered position for a slow count of 3 to 5 before coming back up.*

DOS AND DON'TS

❏ Do not let your heels drop to the floor when coming up.

❏ When lowering your torso, do not allow your buttocks to go below your knees. This would mean putting too much pressure on your knees.

❏ Do not try to aim your knees too far out to the side. Let their position be natural.

❏ Keep your shoulders relaxed.

❏ Do not arch your back or stick out your buttocks. Keep your spine straight and your neck stretched.

❏ If you don't have time to do 20 reps, you can do 10 in even slower motion for the same effect.

❏ The slower you do this exercise, the stronger your front thigh muscles will become.

❏ The more erect your torso, the more your thigh muscles are worked.

HAMSTRING STRETCH #1
Up and Over

While doing the standing hamstring stretches, most people take the foot they're standing on directly out to the side (usually for balance). Try to learn to aim the foot forward (train yourself to do this). It is more gentle on the knees.

(If you have sciatica, always keep your knees bent during this exercise, to relieve pressure on your lower back.)

❑ Standing straight, take your right leg up and rest your heel on your barre or piece of furniture. Your left foot should be turned out slightly for balance, with your left knee straight but relaxed.

❑ Stretch your torso and arms up towards the ceiling. Still stretching up, slowly round your torso over your right leg.

❑ When you're over as far as you can go, crisscross your hands, letting them rest lightly on your right ankle. Take your elbows out to the side and rest your head on your leg. Do not lock your knees.

Feel the beautiful stretch.

IF YOU WANT MORE OF A STRETCH: *Once you're in position, try to put your head in between the left side of your right leg and the crook of your arm.*

This is a lovely stretch for your neck and spine.

If that's too difficult or you're not quite stretched enough, you can move your hands up a little bit higher on your right leg, and rest your forehead on your leg, wherever it's comfortable (except directly on your kneecap).

❏ Gently move your torso up and down, 1/16 to 1/4 inch, or just hold the position.

50 REPS

❏ To come out of this exercise, slowly round your torso up, and gently take your right leg to the floor in *triple slow motion*.

❏ Repeat this exercise on the opposite side.

50 REPS

REMEMBER: *A lot of people, especially women, have knees that bulge quite a bit on the inside of their legs. To make this area thinner and smoother, gently turn your raised leg and foot out to the side slightly—your right leg to the right or your left leg to the left.*

DOS AND DON'TS

❏ It doesn't matter how high your barre is. If you want more of a stretch, gently take your standing leg back, *away* from the barre. (And *never* use a towel rack for a barre! They are not designed to hold your weight! Make sure whatever you use for a barre can support your weight.)

❏ If resting your heel on your barre or piece of furniture is uncomfortable, place a facecloth under your ankle.

❏ Do not turn the foot you're standing on directly out to the side—unless that is the only way you can keep your balance—and keep that knee relaxed.

❏ Keep your hips even.

❏ Keep your elbows bent and stretched out.

❏ Relax your body.

❏ Take advantage of the time you have to relax your neck during this exercise.

❏ Do not force your stretch.

❏ Do not lock your knees.

❏ No bouncing.

Hamstring Stretch #2
Bent Leg

THIS IS A STRETCH TO BE RESPECTED!

REMEMBER: *If you are standing on a slippery floor and feel that you are about to slip, you can place a suction-cup–type of rubber bath mat under your foot so you don't slide forward under the barre.*

❏ Gently place the arch of your right foot up on your barre or piece of furniture, with your right knee bent. (The back of a sofa or heavy chair is excellent to use as a barre for this exercise.) Place both hands on your barre, each on either side of your foot. Keep the foot you are standing on in whatever position is most comfortable, and bend your left knee slightly. Slowly scoot forward as far as you can on your standing foot, then aim that same foot towards the barre as much as you can.

❏ Crisscross your hands over your right foot, and hold onto the barre.

❏ In triple slow motion, straighten your right leg as far as you can without forcing, which will automatically straighten your left leg. Do not lock your standing knee. Do not force it. Stretch your elbows out to the sides as far as you can, and rest your head on your right leg.

Notice how both legs have been straightened, but they are completely relaxed. Never lock your knees.

HOLD FOR A COUNT OF 50

FOR MORE OF A STRETCH: *Place your head to the right side of your leg.*
You can also bend your left leg and at the same time gently move up and down, just a few inches.

Here the left leg is bent slightly. The elbows are still stretched out to the sides as far as they can go. And see how relaxed the neck and head are.

FOR EVEN MORE OF A STRETCH: *You can place your head to the left side of your leg.*

For an even stronger stretch, gently slide your right foot down slightly so that your heel is underneath the barre.

You can also rotate your left hip out and to the back, while your heel remains underneath the barre. This stretches your buttocks and hip muscles.

This is the correct position if you choose to rotate your left hip out and to the back. Notice how the torso has shifted over very slightly to the left.

❏ To come out of this exercise, first bend the leg you're standing on and uncross your hands. Then, slowly and gently, take your right leg off your barre or piece of furniture and, in triple slow motion, lower it to the floor.

❏ Repeat this exercise on the opposite side.

HOLD FOR A COUNT OF 50

DOS AND DON'TS

❑ Never force your leg to straighten more than it comfortably can.

❑ Do not overstretch.

❑ Keep your body relaxed.

❑ Relax the leg you're standing on, even though it's straight. Do not tighten that knee.

❑ Do not bounce.

❑ Do not tense your arms.

❑ Keep your neck relaxed.

❑ Think beautiful, soft thoughts.

LEG STRENGTHENER
Knee Bends in the Air

❏ Stand at your barre or piece of furniture, and hold it gently for balance. Bend your right leg out to the side, sliding your right foot up your left leg until your toes are pointing on your left knee. Bend your left knee slightly.

Keep your body relaxed. Do not lock your standing knee.

❑ Straighten your right leg out—halfway between the front and the side of your body—as high as it can go.

Keep your shoulders relaxed.

❑ Bend your right knee in again taking it higher towards the ceiling and being certain not to let your toes return to your left knee. Your toes are pointed and relaxed. From that position, straighten your leg up even higher.

Raise your leg progressively higher each time. But only go as high as you can without forcing.

❏ Bend your right knee in a third time, then straighten your leg, taking it even higher—as high as you can—towards the ceiling. This time, when you straighten your leg as high as it will go, *keep* it straightened (but *never* lock your knee), and gently, in triple slow motion, move your leg up and down 1/16 to 1/4 inch.

5 TO 10 REPS

REMEMBER: *Each time you straighten your right leg, you should try to raise it a little bit higher.*

❏ Then, if you choose, keeping your left knee slightly bent, raise yourself up on the toes of your left foot, and do the remaining reps on your toes.

If you choose to go up on your toes, remember that your leg extension will not be as great. You will, however, be strengthening the leg and buttocks muscles of your standing leg at the same time as you are stretching your right leg as high as you can take it.

5 TO 10 REPS ON YOUR TOES

❏ To come out of this exercise, bend your right knee, pointing your toes in towards your left knee. Then, in triple slow motion, lower your right leg to the floor.

❏ Repeat this exercise on the opposite side.

DOS AND DON'TS

❏ If you find the amount of reps to be a bit more than you can do at first, start off with 2 to 3 reps with your standing foot flat and 2 to 3 on your toes, gradually working up to 10 reps total. When your legs become stronger, you will be able to do all the reps with your standing leg remaining straight.

❏ Do not lock your knees.

❏ Do not lower your leg as you extend it out.

❏ Do not drop your head.

❏ Keep your neck and your shoulders relaxed.

❏ Do not arch your back.

❏ Keep your torso erect.

❏ Use your barre only for balance.

❏ Relax your legs.

BUTTOCKS– OUTER THIGHS–HIPS

(If you have knee problems, substitute the Sitting or Standing exercises in this section for the Kneeling exercises.)

(If you have a swayback, always round your shoulders as much as you can, or, if you feel it's necessary, you can also let your torso lean over to the opposite side of the leg being used, when doing the exercises in this section. This will stretch the spine even more.)

At this advanced point, you should know how to really curl your pelvis up. The more you curl it up, especially on the Kneeling and Standing exercises of this section, the more your muscles can contract and work, the more your outer thighs will become tight, and the faster you will get those darling round, little peach buttocks!

Also, most of you should be so adept at rolling your hip forward in the starting position that you won't even have to think about using your hand to assist you.

And you should not have to be reminded not to wear shoes for any of the Buttocks—Outer Thighs—Hips exercises. The weight of them is simply too heavy.

REMEMBER: *The more your hip is rolled forward for these first 2 sitting exercises (and the Kneeling Out to the Side exercise), the more you will be working your buttocks muscles.*

Sitting Bringing Up the Rear

This exercise begins in the same starting position as Bringing Up the Rear in *Callanetics Countdown*, or in Behind and Hips in *Callanetics—The One-Hour Program* and *Callanetics for Your Back*—except this time you will be positioning the leg you're resting on further out to the side.

❑ Sitting on the floor or a mat to cushion yourself if necessary, place your hands on whatever you're using as a barre and rest them there lightly. The height does not matter, as long as you are comfortable. Your left knee is bent in front of you. Your right knee is bent and even with your right hip. Your right foot rests on the floor behind you. Still holding onto your barre, move your left knee over to the left 3 to 5 inches, and take your left foot out a little for a balance point.

❑ Making sure that your right hip remains facing the barre, roll it forward as far as you can. As the hip is rolled forward, the torso automatically turns to the left. Your foot will come off the floor.

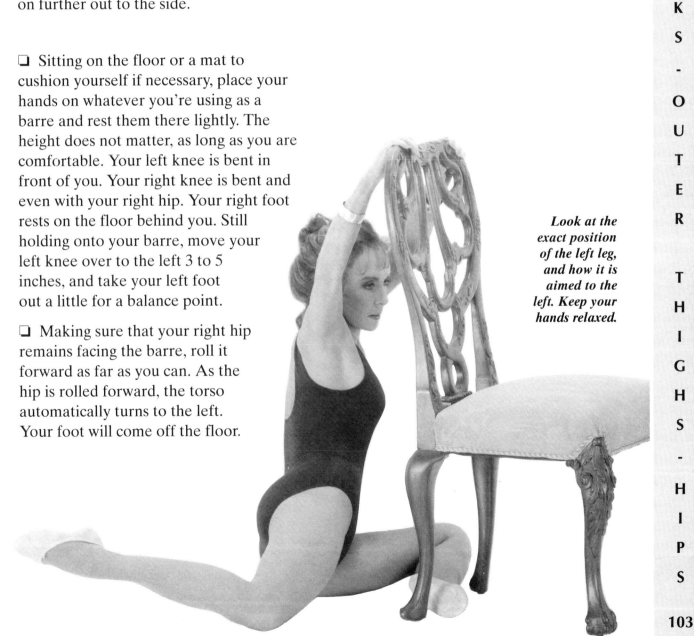

Look at the exact position of the left leg, and how it is aimed to the left. Keep your hands relaxed.

103

B U T T O C K S - O U T E R T H I G H S - H I P S

❏ Lift your right knee off the floor. Slowly rotate your kneecap so that it is aiming towards the ceiling as much as possible. This will keep your knee and foot on exactly the same level, 1 to 3 inches off the floor.

When your muscles become extremely strong, you'll be able to roll your hip forward even more, causing your knee to be so low that it will almost seem to be brushing the floor.

❏ Move your knee in triple slow motion back and forth, 1/16 to 1/4 inch.

100 REPS

IF YOU WANT MORE OF A WORKOUT FOR YOUR BUTTOCKS: *Lower your foot a little bit, and aim your kneecap even more towards the ceiling, but do not let your hip rotate to the back.*

For even more of a workout in this same position, you can also lift your knee and foot a wee bit more.

104

WHEN THIS EXERCISE BECOMES TOO EASY: *Be sure to sit more erect. You can also raise your barre, or place your hands higher up on your piece of furniture. The higher the barre, the more intense this exercise becomes.*

IF YOU FEEL IT'S TOO MUCH, AND YOUR BODY IS BEGINNING TO TENSE UP:
Take a breather, then roll back into position.

You can also switch sides, but be sure to do a proper count for both sides before continuing this section.

You can also bring your knee forward a wee bit.

❏ Relax your entire body, then repeat this exercise on the opposite side.

100 REPS

Dos and Don'ts

❑ Do not arch your lower back.

❑ Relax your legs.

❑ Relax your neck.

❑ The movement back and forth is almost imperceptible.

❑ Do not allow the foot of your working leg to rest on the floor. If it starts to feel heavy, take a breather.

❑ Do not take the knee of your working leg past your hip when you are returning forward during the little motions.

❑ Relax your shoulders. If you feel pressure on your lower back, you have 3 choices:
   ❑ Round your shoulders more;
   ❑ Lean over to the opposite side of your working leg just a wee bit, keeping your back straight; or
   ❑ Tighten your buttocks and curl your pelvis up.
   Some people choose to do all 3 in one go at first.

❑ Do not allow your torso to push forward when you are rolling your *hip* forward. This will put pressure on your lower back. Keep your torso erect but relaxed.

❑ Keep your hips even.

❑ Relax even more!

Sitting Out to the Side

❏ Still seated with your hands up on your barre, bend your left leg out on the floor in front of you. Relax your shoulders.

❏ Move your left knee 3 to 5 inches to the left. Fully extend your right leg out, straight, directly to the side, even with your hip. Then slowly roll your right hip and leg over so that the tops of your toes are aiming into the floor (if possible). Bring your right leg in towards your body. Because your right leg can move in 3 to 4 inches, this will automatically take your hips to the left, causing you to lean slightly to the left.

Rolling the hip forward automatically turns the torso to the left and gives the appearance that the working leg has been taken further back. How deceiving appearances can be!

❏ Gently lift your right leg up and down,
1/16 to 1/4 inch.

100 REPS

❏ Repeat this exercise on the opposite side.

100 REPS

Notice how very little the foot is raised up off the floor. The movement can remain so small because the hip has been rolled over so much.

WHEN THIS EXERCISE BECOMES TOO EASY: *Take your working leg to the back without rotating your hip back. You can also sit more erect.*

IF THIS EXERCISE IS BECOMING TOO DIFFICULT: *Slowly ease your working leg forward a few inches. You can also lean directly over to the opposite side.*

DOS AND DON'TS

❏ Keep your extended leg very straight, but do not lock your knee.

❏ Do not allow your torso to push forward. This will put pressure on your lower back.

❏ Keep your working hip rolled forward as much as you can.

❏ If you feel pressure on your lower back, you have 3 choices:
   ❏ Round your torso;
   ❏ Lean over to the opposite side of your working leg just a wee bit; or
   ❏ Tighten your buttocks and curl your pelvis up more than you think you can.

❏ Never arch your back.

❏ If you are in the most advanced position for this exercise, you will only be able to lift your leg 1/16 to 1/4 inch. If you are not yet strong enough for this, you may lean your torso a wee bit to the left and lift your leg higher—but make sure it is no higher than 2 inches off the floor. Otherwise, because you may be tired, you might turn your leg towards the ceiling, and begin working the front thigh muscles instead of the buttocks.

Kneeling Bringing Up the Rear

Even though I know I keep saying 'Round your upper back,' when your muscles become strong enough and you can do the famous pelvic curl-up as second nature, many of you will have noticed that you no longer have to round your upper back during these kneeling exercises.

REMEMBER: *Whenever you tighten your buttocks and curl your pelvis up, your working leg will automatically come forward. Be sure to take your leg back, keeping your knee even with your hip, to get the full benefit of this exercise. The fact that you're taking your knee back does not mean that the hip of that same leg has to move! Be sure, however, that your pelvis stays curled up.*

❏ Kneeling, with knees together and both hands resting loosely on your barre or piece of furniture, arms straight but relaxed, rotate your body, including your legs, to the left. Tighten your buttocks, curl your pelvis up, and round your upper back.

❏ In triple slow motion, take your right knee out to the side and up towards the ceiling as high as it can go without lifting your right foot. When the knee will not go up any further, rotate your kneecap so that it is aiming up towards the ceiling and curl your pelvis up even more than you think you can. Then take your knee up even higher, allowing your foot to lift off the floor as you do so. Because your right knee came forward when you turned your body, now take your knee back as far as you can without moving your right hip or arching your lower back.

❏ Take your left hip towards the left very slightly to distribute your weight off your kneecap.

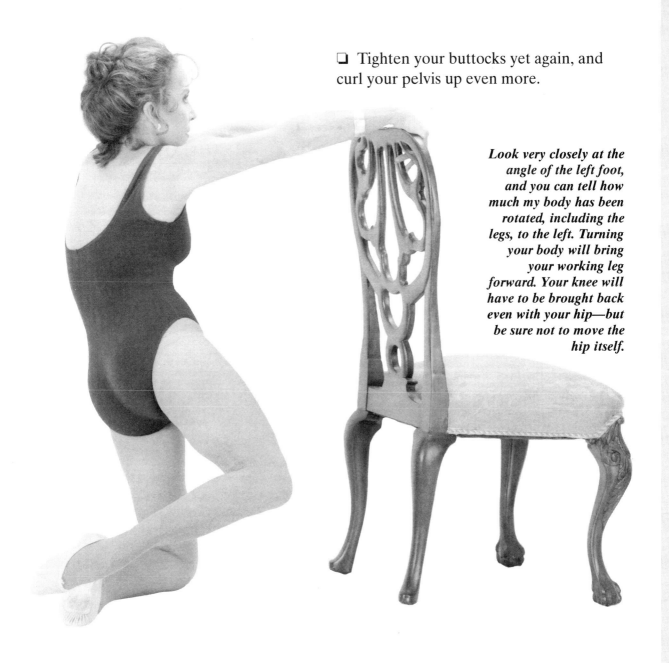

❏ Tighten your buttocks yet again, and curl your pelvis up even more.

Look very closely at the angle of the left foot, and you can tell how much my body has been rotated, including the legs, to the left. Turning your body will bring your working leg forward. Your knee will have to be brought back even with your hip—but be sure not to move the hip itself.

❏ Gently move your right leg back and forth, no more than 1/16 to 1/4 inch.

100 REPS

❏ Repeat this exercise on the opposite side.

100 REPS

DOS AND DON'TS

❑ Really tip your pelvis up more than you think you can.

❑ Always make sure that your lower back is straight and relaxed, and that your buttocks are not sticking out.

❑ If you feel pressure on your lower back, round your shoulders even more.

❑ Don't move your hip when taking your working leg back and forth. Aim with your knee, going back and forth in tiny little movements. Try to keep your knee aimed up towards the ceiling, and don't let it go in front of the line of your hip.

This is the absolute **wrong** *way to do this exercise. Shoulders tense . . . lower back arched . . . body not turned . . . buttocks not tightened or pelvis curled up . . . weight of body on kneecap . . . knee not rotated up towards the ceiling. Terrible!*

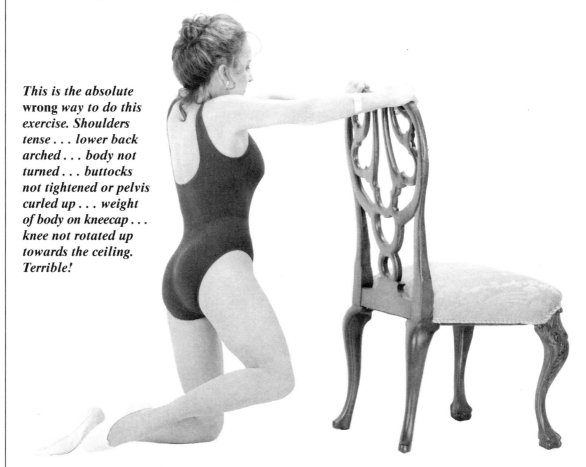

❑ Relax your shoulders, keeping them rounded.

❑ Be certain to shift your weight directly off your kneecap. You can place a towel or exercise mat under your knee, if you like.

Kneeling Out to the Side

❏ Kneeling, with both hands on your barre or piece of furniture, stretch your right leg straight out to the side, even with your hip.

❏ Rotate your right leg forward, until the top of your toes rest on the floor, if possible. (This is more of a rotation than in the one-hour Callanetics program.) Allowing your hips to move to the left, bring your right leg in towards your body so that you won't be putting pressure on your kneecap.

❏ Tighten your buttocks, and curl your pelvis up more than you ever thought you could. Round your upper back. Make sure your lower back is straight, not arched, and relaxed.

Because of the angle of the chair, it appears that I have taken the right leg back. The leg here is actually even with the hip.

❏ Gently lift your right leg, up and down, in a smooth and tiny motion, 1/16 to 1/4 inch.

100 REPS

IF THIS EXERCISE IS BECOMING TOO DIFFICULT: *Take a breather. If your working leg is starting to feel too heavy, take it a wee bit forward. You can also lean your torso over to the side opposite your working leg. Remember to breathe naturally. If you do take a breather, be sure to get into the original starting position before continuing the exercise.*

❏ Repeat this exercise on the opposite side.

100 REPS

DOS AND DON'TS

❏ Keep the top of your back rounded, as if you were a cat. Do not arch your lower back; keep it perfectly straight.

❏ Keep your pelvis tipped up more than you think you can.

❏ Relax your body as much as you can, from head to toe, especially your shoulders and neck.

❏ Keep your working leg straight, but your knee remains relaxed. Never lock your knee.

❏ Do not ever place your full weight directly on your kneecap. Place a towel or exercise mat under your knee, if you like.

❏ Do not stick out your buttocks.

Standing Bringing Up the Rear

THIS EXERCISE WAS DRAWN FROM A POSITION IN CLASSICAL BALLET CALLED AN *attitude.*

❏ Stand at your barre or piece of furniture, your hands resting lightly on it for balance, elbows bent. Your feet are together.

❏ In triple slow motion, lift your right knee and take it up and out to the side as high as you can without moving your right hip up or forward. Keep your right knee even with your right hip. Your right foot will automatically come off the floor when you lift your knee.

❏ Point your foot to the rear, and keep it relaxed. It should always be lower than your knees.

❏ Bend your left knee slightly, the one you're standing on. Tighten your buttocks, and curl your pelvis up. Round your shoulders. Your knee may go forward, so carefully take it back, even with your hip—but don't *move* your hip.

❏ Bend sideways at the waist and aim your right shoulder towards the floor. Relax your shoulders and neck.

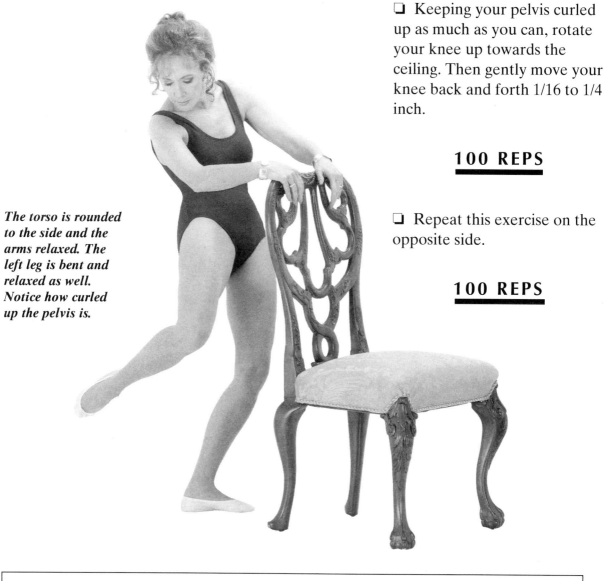

The torso is rounded to the side and the arms relaxed. The left leg is bent and relaxed as well. Notice how curled up the pelvis is.

❏ Keeping your pelvis curled up as much as you can, rotate your knee up towards the ceiling. Then gently move your knee back and forth 1/16 to 1/4 inch.

100 REPS

❏ Repeat this exercise on the opposite side.

100 REPS

DOS AND DON'TS

❏ Make sure your lower back is stretched. Do not arch your back at all.

❏ Keep your hips even.

❏ Relax your shoulders and your neck.

❏ Do not lock your knees.

❏ Make sure the leg you're standing on is slightly bent.

❏ Relax your entire body—and stay relaxed!

Standing Out to the Side

THIS EXERCISE WAS ALSO DRAWN FROM A POSITION IN CLASSICAL BALLET CALLED AN *arabesque.*

This is one exercise I definitely take advantage of while standing having a conversation with someone. When you become stronger, you will not have to hold onto anything! The movement is so ridiculously tiny that no one ever knows I'm even doing it. At that level, you should keep your torso straight and relaxed.

❏ Stand at your barre or piece of furniture, your hands resting lightly on it for balance. Your feet are together.

❏ Take your right leg directly out to the side, even with your hip, pointing your toes like a ballet dancer's but keeping them relaxed. They should be aiming forward. Your leg is straight, but your knee remains relaxed. Bend your left knee slightly.

❑ Allowing your hips to move to the left, bring your right leg in towards your body. It can usually come in about 4 to 6 inches.

❑ Tighten your buttocks and curl your pelvis up.

❑ Bend at the waist and aim your right shoulder towards the floor.

Don't forget to take your body over to the opposite side of the leg you're working on. You can see how relaxed the entire body is. Notice that the right leg is straight and relaxed.

❑ Tighten your buttocks and curl your pelvis up even more than you think you can.

❑ Gently start moving your leg up and down, 1/16 to 1/4 inch.

100 REPS

❏ Repeat this exercise on the opposite side.

100 REPS

DOS AND DON'TS

❏ Keep your shoulders relaxed; they should be doing absolutely nothing.

❏ Keep your hips even. They should not be moving at all.

❏ Do not arch your back.

❏ Always keep the pelvis tipped up more than you think you can.

❏ If you feel you're losing your position and your arms are taking over, take a breather. Or you can take the working leg forward a wee bit.

❏ Do not lock your knees.

❏ Keep your working leg straight, but do not lock its knee.

THE
ENTIRE BODY

Open and Close

This exercise builds up incredible strength throughout the entire body. In ballet school, before classes, some students and I would do Open and Close for stamina, leg strength, and for a higher extension of the leg. At the beginning, the more you do, the lower your legs will go. Expect this—don't think you're not doing this exercise correctly if it happens! Believe it or not, there are some people in their seventies who can do fifty Open and Closes effortlessly, without breathers, and their legs remain at the same height.

But as with so much of Super Callanetics, this is an exercise that must be respected. Most people with back problems have found that Open and Close has helped their backs tremendously—because they knew their own limitations and did not force the exercise. This means they *stopped* when they felt that the lower back was about to take over, and only did what they felt they could do *properly* at that particular time.

And as you should be aware from the one-hour program, even though this is basically a leg exercise, it requires tremendous use of the stomach muscles as well. This is why, if your abdominals are not particularly strong, your lower back will inevitably take over—which is not what you want! Build yourself up slowly, and you'll soon find that another wonderful benefit of this exercise is that your stomach muscles also become stronger.

REMEMBER: *If you feel you're losing strength, or your lower back is about to take over, lower your legs a few inches, or bend your knees as you open and close. Or take a breather. If you find that you're still feeling pressure on your lower back, you must discontinue this exercise until you have built up more strength in your stomach and leg muscles.*

REMEMBER: *Height does not matter. Work at your own level. All of the Green Beret and Special Forces that I taught in Berlin discovered in horror that they couldn't even lift their legs off the floor! They had to drag them back and forth across the floor (no comment!).*

BUT DON'T FORGET: *Open and Close must be treated with the respect it deserves!*

❑ Sit on a mat with your upper back against a sofa or counter, and hold onto it as if there is a barre above your head. (Some people use a chest of drawers with one drawer open in place of a barre.) If you have a barre, sit under it with your hands or wrists draped lightly atop it. (By this time, you shouldn't find yourself holding onto it for dear life!)

❑ Bend your knees and take them up towards your chest. Point your toes. Scoot your buttocks forward a few inches so that you are not sitting on your tailbone. Gently drop your chin. This will help stretch your spine more.

You should be totally relaxed when starting this exercise.

❏ Slowly, straighten your legs, without locking your knees, pointing your toes up towards the ceiling as high as you can without forcing. You are sitting in a jackknife position.

❏ In triple slow motion, open your legs as wide as you can, and then close them.

It takes incredible strength for your legs to go this high with ease. Work at your own pace.

DO 5 SETS OF 10, 2 SETS OF 25, OR 50 REPS

❏ To come out of this exercise, gently bend your knees in the closed position, bringing your legs in close to your body, and lower them to the floor.

REMEMBER: *At this point in Super Callanetics, you should already be able to do 50 continuous reps. If, however, you need to break them into 2 sets to avoid putting pressure on your lower back, please do so.*

Some people do Open and Close in sets of 10.

DOS AND DON'TS

❏ If your muscles are not particularly strong, stop and take breathers, and gradually work up to a set of 25, increasing slowly as your muscles tighten and strengthen.

❏ The closer you can place your buttocks up against a wall or piece of furniture, the more difficult this exercise. It is much harder to raise your legs when you are sitting that way—just try one and you'll understand—and as you know, the higher you can raise your legs, the harder Open and Close becomes.

❏ Take as many breathers as you wish.

❏ Your body must stay relaxed. Do not tighten your grip on the barre or furniture.

❏ Always make sure that the object you're holding onto is sturdy enough to hold your weight (without your having to worry about it!).

❏ Relax your legs, especially the knees; eventually they will be light as feathers.

❏ Keep your chin down.

❏ Although your toes are pointed, keep your feet relaxed.

❏ Never force your legs to move more than they can.

STRETCHES

(If you have sciatic pain, always keep your knees bent during all of these stretches. This will help relieve the pressure. If that is not helpful, discontinue these stretches until it is better.)

Sitting Inner-Thigh Stretch

❏ Sitting on the floor, stretch your legs out so they are spread as far apart as they can be without forcing. Place your hands either in front or in back of you—whichever you prefer—and gently push your pelvis into the floor.

Keep your torso relaxed. Never force your legs farther than they can go.

❏ Stretch your torso up, then gently stretch your arms out behind you, and clasp your hands, as you did in the Standing Hamstring Stretch, on page 48.

❏ In triple slow motion, round your upper back forward until your head and shoulders are down as far as they can go without straining. (If you are very stretched, you should be able to touch the floor with either your face, your nose, or your upper torso.)

❏ Gently let your arms move even higher behind your back; try to stretch your torso so that your arms are aiming directly up towards the ceiling.

Move your arms up as high as you can without forcing.

❏ Relax your body, and feel the stretch in your lower back and inner thighs. If you are stretched enough to be resting on the floor, however, simply take advantage of this time to let your body melt into the floor, especially your neck. (This stretch can be so relaxing—careful that you don't fall asleep!)

HOLD FOR A COUNT OF 50

❏ Or, if you are *not* resting on the floor, gently move your torso 1/16 to 1/4 inch, up and down.

50 REPS TO THE CENTER

❏ Next you will be going over to your right leg. Unclasp your hands and slowly take your torso over to your right leg, bringing your arms over at the same time. (Or, if you prefer, you may walk your hands over in front of you on the floor.)

❏ Lower your hands lightly and crisscross them on your ankle, taking your elbows out and forward to stretch your waist. (It's the opposite arm going forward that stretches your waist.) Let your head rest on your leg.

Try to keep your elbows out and away from your body to stretch between your shoulder blades. Keep your neck relaxed.

❏ In an almost imperceptible motion, gently move your head and torso towards your feet or the floor, 1/16 to 1/4 inch, and then back.

50 REPS TO THE RIGHT

129

❏ Gently walk your hands over to your outstretched left leg, and again crisscross them to rest on your ankle. Let your head rest on your leg.

❏ Delicately move back and forth, 1/16 to 1/4 inch.

50 REPS TO THE LEFT

❏ To come out of this exercise, in triple slow motion, gently walk your hands up your leg (do not touch your knee) or place your hands on either side of your leg and walk your hands up as you roll your torso back up to the starting position, vertebra by vertebra.

FOR MORE OF A STRETCH ON EACH SIDE: *Keep your elbows out away from your body. The more you aim your elbows forward, the more you will be stretching your waist. You can also rest your head on either side of your leg, then move gently back and forth towards your foot.*

DOS AND DON'TS

❏ Do not force your body down.

❏ Do feel the stretch in your lower back and inner thighs—*feel* the waist stretch when you're over to the side.

❏ Do not bounce.

❏ Do not pull forward with your neck.

❏ Relax your toes and your legs.

❏ Relax your entire body, especially your neck.

Sitting Hamstring Stretch

(If you have sciatica, always keep your knees bent during this exercise.)

This is the stretch I do when I feel like my neck is becoming like a brick (not even crumbling!) from stress. It should be able to help you as well.

   This is basically the same movement forward as the Sitting Inner-Thigh Stretch, done with your legs together.

❑ Sitting up on the floor, close your legs so that your feet are together in front of you, pointed but relaxed.

FOR MORE OF A STRETCH: *Especially for your calves, turn your feet up so they are flexed.*

❑ Stretch your arms out behind you, and clasp your hands. Now gently raise them up as high as you can take them.

❑ Stretch your torso up, then slowly round your upper torso forward until your head and shoulders are down as far as they can go without forcing. Feel the stretch in your lower back as you go down. Try to rest your head on your legs.

❏ Let your arms move up gently even higher behind your back; try to stretch your torso so that your arms are aiming directly up towards the ceiling.

People have become so relaxed in this position that some of them feel like taking a nap!

❏ Relax your body, and feel the stretch in your lower back and hamstrings.

❏ Gently move your torso 1/16 to 1/4 inch, up and down, if you are not resting your head on your legs. If you are stretched enough to be resting on your legs, however, simply take advantage of this time to let your body melt into your legs, especially your neck. Or, if you prefer, you can gently move your head towards your feet, forward and back, 1/16 to 1/4 inch.

HOLD FOR A COUNT OF 50

❏ To come out of this stretch, bring your arms down in triple slow motion, unclasp your hands, and rest them on the floor.

❏ Slowly bring your body up, rounding your torso, one vertebra at a time.

Dos and Don'ts

❏ Your torso is rounded—not straight—when you're going down. Otherwise you'll be putting pressure on your lower back.

❏ Relax your legs, especially your knees.

❏ Relax your neck and shoulders. Allow your neck to melt into the floor.

❏ Do not force your body down.

❏ Do feel this stretch in your lower back.

Lying-Down Hamstring and Calf Stretch

(If you have sciatica, always keep your knees bent during this exercise, to relieve pressure on your lower back.)

❏ Lie on your back and bend your knees. Keep your feet flat on the floor.

❏ Bend your right knee up into your chest, and then straighten that leg.

❏ Clasp your hands around your calf or ankle with your elbows up and out, and, in triple slow motion, bring your leg as close to your body as you can.

❏ Gently straighten your left leg on the floor, without locking your knee, and rest your left heel on the floor.

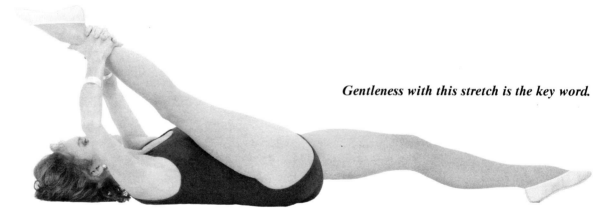

Gentleness with this stretch is the key word.

❏ With an almost imperceptible motion, move your right leg towards your body, 1/16 to 1/4 inch.

50 REPS

FOR MORE OF A STRETCH, OR TO STRETCH YOUR CALVES: *Flex your feet towards you. Do not point them up towards the ceiling.*

❏ To come out of this stretch, bend both your knees in a smooth, gentle motion, and place your feet flat on the floor. Bring your arms down as well, and rest them by your side.

❏ Repeat this exercise on the opposite side.

50 REPS

DOS AND DON'TS

❏ Do not force your leg up higher than it can go.

❏ Do not lock your knees.

❏ Keep the leg that is resting on the floor as straight and as low as possible, as long as your knee remains relaxed.

❏ Keep the foot of your raised leg pointed but relaxed.

❏ Do not tighten your grasp on your calf or ankle.

❏ Keep your neck and shoulders very relaxed. Take advantage of this time to relax your neck and entire body.

Spine Stretch

Remember in the one-hour Callanetics program I explained that this was a gentle adaptation of a chiropractic manipulation—and that after doing the Spine Stretch, my hips became even for the first time in my life? Well, nearly twenty years later, my hips are *still* even . . . but of course I always take advantage of this spine stretch as much as I can.

❑ Still lying on the floor with your knees bent and feet resting flat, bring your arms up to your shoulders.

❑ Bending from the elbow, place your forearms at a right angle to the side of your head, resting them lightly with your palms facing upward. Your elbows must remain on the floor.

❑ In triple slow motion, lift your right knee, bent, up to your chest. Let your left leg gently ease down until it rests on the floor. Take your bent right knee over to your left side, away from your body as much as you can, trying to rest your foot and knee on the floor.

Notice the position of the left leg, resting on the floor—and how far back it has been taken for even more of a stretch. Both knees are very relaxed.

FOR MORE OF A STRETCH: *Gently move your right knee up to your left elbow.*

FOR EVEN MORE OF A STRETCH: *Ease your straight leg to the back of you, as shown in the photo above.*

HOLD FOR A COUNT OF 50 TO 100

❑ To come out of this stretch and go over to the other side, in triple slow motion, keeping your right knee bent, bring it back to your chest and then place your right foot on the floor, with your knee bent.

❑ Bend your left knee to your chest, and then slide your right foot down to the floor. This is all done in one smooth, continuous motion.

❑ Repeat this stretch on the opposite side.

HOLD FOR A COUNT OF 50 TO 100

❑ To come out of this stretch, in triple slow motion, keeping your left knee bent, bring it back to your chest, and then place your left foot on the floor. Bend your right knee, and place that foot flat on the floor. Then ease yourself up to a standing position in the same manner as you did after the stomach exercises **or** if you are able to, or if you choose to, you can go directly into the Leg Splits.

DOS AND DON'TS

❑ Do not force your bent leg down to the floor.

❑ Do not lift your shoulders or elbows off the floor.

❑ Do keep your body completely relaxed.

❑ Do take advantage of this time to relax your neck.

❑ Remember, gravity is doing the work, not you!

❑ Think beautiful, happy thoughts!

Leg Splits

❏ Moving directly from the end position of the Spine Stretch, roll over and ease yourself up into a sitting position. Extend your right leg in front of you, with your hands resting on the floor to the sides of your right leg.

❏ Extend your left leg as straight behind you as you can.

Do not attempt this until you feel you are very stretched. And then be very careful.

FOR MORE OF A STRETCH: *Bring your torso down to your outstretched right leg, allowing your head to rest on your leg. Keep your elbows out and your arms relaxed, or crisscross your hands over your ankle.*

HOLD FOR A COUNT OF 25

❏ To come out of the split, raise your torso slightly by walking your hands either up your leg or on the floor to the sides of your leg. Bend your right knee and slide it in towards your body. Bend your left leg as well and slide it forward.

❏ Gently ease yourself up by putting your hands on the floor and then gently returning to a standing position, vertebra by vertebra.

Dos and Don'ts

❏ Do only as much of a split as you can.

❏ Do not ever try to force your body down further than it can go. If you can only do a partial split, that's perfectly all right.

❏ Keep your upper body relaxed.

❏ If you are not able to rest both legs straight on the floor, don't worry! You can use your hands to support your body by resting them by your sides, gently on the floor. Be sure, however, not to push into the floor (this is a stretch, not a push-up!).

PELVIS—
FRONT AND INNER
THIGHS

Pelvic Rotation

(If you have knee problems, you can do the Pelvic Rotation in a standing position, with your knees bent. You will not see results as quickly, but as you already know, your health and safety are far more important!)

As most of you already will have experienced from the one-hour program, the reason the Pelvic Rotation is such a challenge is because it helps you gather strength from your entire body (including your toes!). As one student commented in class, 'It's excitingly frightening how much your pelvis can curl up!'

❏ On a mat, sit comfortably on your heels. Your knees are together and your legs relaxed.

❏ Stretch your arms up over your head and clasp your hands together. Keep your torso erect, and feel the stretch in your back.

❏ Lift your torso 2 to 3 inches up off your heels.

❏ Take your right hip over to the right side as far as you can. Roll your pelvis forward, to the front, at the same time curling it up and aiming it into your navel. Move your left hip over to the left side as far as you can. Then move your buttocks to the back, completing a circle.

The entire routine is one continuous slow motion.

The motion is a smooth, flowing circle—hip—pelvis—hip—behind.
Only your pelvis moves in an unbroken circle.

20 REPS OF A CIRCLE,
STARTING WITH YOUR RIGHT HIP OVER TO THE SIDE

❑ Take a breather for a few seconds, then lift yourself back into position, feeling the stretch in your lower back.

❑ Repeat the Pelvic Rotation, starting to the left.

20 REPS OF A CIRCLE,
STARTING WITH YOUR LEFT
HIP OVER TO THE SIDE

Your pelvis can curl up more than you think it can.

DOS AND DON'TS

❏ Whichever Callanetics you have been doing, at this point you should be able to make a larger, more flowing circle. The Super Callanetics Pelvic Rotation allows you to aim your buttocks back, because you should have more flexibility in that area by now, and can complete a full circle without difficulty. This is not an up-and-down motion with your pelvis but a smooth circular motion. Do not ever allow your movements to become jerky—they should always flow.

From this angle, you can see how I have taken my buttocks to the back to complete the circle.

❏ Do keep your entire body relaxed.

❏ The more you can curl your pelvis up into your navel, the more effective this exercise.

❏ Take breathers whenever you feel it necessary.

❏ Most men find it difficult to sit directly on the bottom of their feet. They can either turn both ankles out towards the floor—this creates a nice little hollow space for their buttocks to rest in. Or they can place the bottom of their toes on the floor and sit on their heels, which would then be facing up towards the ceiling.

Pelvic Rotation—Figure 8

Learn to master this rotation—it will give you incredible control of your pelvic area.

This exercise is done in exactly the same manner as the Pelvic Rotation.

❏ Sit on your heels, knees together, your legs relaxed.

❏ Lift your arms up over your head and clasp your hands together. Feel the stretch in your lower back, and keep your torso erect.

❏ Lift your torso 2 to 3 inches up off your heels.

❏ Take your right hip out to the side, as far as you can. Then roll your right hip forward, aiming it up. As you do this, your left hip will automatically lower a few inches, and be aimed more towards your back.

❏ Then, take your left buttock back as far as it will go. When your left buttock can't go back any further, gently start rounding your left hip forward in a half-circle to the point where your left hip is up and forward as far as it can go. Your right hip is now back.

DO AS MANY AS YOU CAN

The motion is a smooth figure 8—one hip up—the opposite buttock down and back—one hip up—the opposite buttock down and back. Only your pelvis moves.

Dos and Don'ts

❑ You must be terribly strong in your inner
thighs to attempt this figure 8.

❑ Do not arch your back or stick out your
buttocks.

❑ Do keep your body relaxed.

Pelvic Scoop

❑ Kneel on a mat, knees together, with your feet outstretched behind you and your legs relaxed.

❑ Lift your arms up over your head and clasp your hands together. Feel the stretch in your lower back.

❑ Lower your arms in front about a foot. Round your torso a wee bit forward. Now, keeping your spine straight, aim your buttocks down towards your heels. *Do not arch your back.*

Keep your arms and shoulders relaxed and your spine straight.

❏ When you have stretched your buttocks to the point where they are delicately brushing your heels, gently tighten your buttocks, then curl your pelvis up even more than you think you can, in a slow scooping motion.

The stronger you are, the more you will be able to take your arms towards the back when you are scooping back up.

❏ Raise your arms back up till your hands are above your head in the starting position.

❏ Keep curling your pelvis up until you have returned to the original kneeling position.

REMEMBER: *The more you can take your arms and torso back when you are returning to the original kneeling position with your curl-up, the faster your thigh muscles will strengthen. This is, however, quite a challenge.*

And the higher you can curl your pelvis, the more you will be strengthening your inner thighs.

10 TO 20 REPS

FOR MORE OF A CHALLENGE: *Push your knees together when you are returning to the starting position.*

DOS AND DON'TS

❏ **Do keep your entire body relaxed.**

❏ **Do keep your arms and shoulders relaxed. Do not strain your arms forward.**

❏ **Keep your pelvis curled up when you are returning to your original position.**

❏ **Do not arch your back.**

❏ **Keep your buttocks tightened when you are returning to the kneeling position.**

❏ **If you find yourself needing a breather, take one. Relax your body and breathe naturally. Then resume the original position and continue.**

❏ **If you feel a strain in your calves when you are returning to the starting position, bend your arms and torso forward.**

After doing this scoop regularly you will soon be able to relax your calves without thinking about it.

Front-Thigh Stretch

❏ Sit on your heels with your feet relaxed.

❏ Lean back, placing your hands behind you with your palms facing away from your body, and rest your weight on your heels. Relax your neck.

This is the starting position. Keep your knees together and your shoulders relaxed.

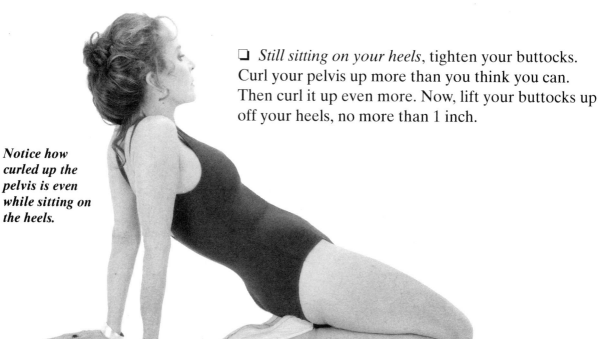

❏ *Still sitting on your heels*, tighten your buttocks. Curl your pelvis up more than you think you can. Then curl it up even more. Now, lift your buttocks up off your heels, no more than 1 inch.

Notice how curled up the pelvis is even while sitting on the heels.

❏ Curl your pelvis up even higher.

Do not lock your elbows. Your arms are straight but relaxed.

❏ Move gently up and down no more than 1/16 to 1/4 inch.

20 REPS

DOS AND DON'TS

❏ Do not arch your back. Keep your spine straight.

❏ Keep your neck relaxed.

❏ Do not move your head up or down.

❏ The more you curl your pelvis up, the more your thighs will stretch.

❏ Do not put too much pressure on your hands.

❏ Relax your entire body.

Inner-Thigh Squeeze

By now, most people will be able to sit erect during this exercise, without putting pressure on their lower backs. If you find that your lower back is still assisting during the Thigh Squeeze, remember to keep your shoulders rounded. You can also take breathers if you need to.

This is also a lovely opportunity to be able to stretch your neck. Let your head lower forward slightly, taking it down in a delicate, slow motion, until your chin is resting on your chest. Or, if you prefer, gently stretch your neck up towards the ceiling.

❏ Facing a chair or legs of a table, sit on the floor, your back straight. Your arms are at your sides, resting lightly on the floor.

❏ Place the arch of each foot on the chair or table legs, up as high as you can keep them without feeling any strain in your lower back. Relax your shoulders.

❏ Keeping your toes pointed and relaxed, squeeze as if trying to bring the legs of your piece of furniture together.

Your inner thighs are doing all the work.

100 REPS • WORK UP TO 300

FOR MORE OF A CHALLENGE: *Place the arches of your feet higher on the outside of the chair or table legs and squeeze.*

For a lovely stretch in the back of your neck, just lower your head.

FOR EVEN MORE OF A CHALLENGE: *With your legs resting on the floor, place the inside of your heels on the outside of the chair or table legs. Point your toes away from the chair or table legs, and squeeze with your heels.*

DOS AND DON'TS

❏ **Keep your shoulders relaxed.**

❏ **Keep your legs relaxed.**

❏ **Do not lock your knees.**

❏ **Relax your lower back.**

❏ **Keep your hands and arms relaxed and comfortable.**

THE
TWENTY-MINUTE
SUPER CALLANETICS
ROUTINE

The Twenty-Minute Super Callanetics Routine

When I am very rushed and don't have time to do the entire Super Callanetics routine, I still allow myself twenty minutes to do some of the exercises. These will still give me strength, stamina, and flexibility throughout my body. (I would be so horrified if my muscles and skin started to sag—anywhere!)

These exercises are what I choose to do in twenty minutes, but *remember,* my muscles are extremely strong, so I can breeze through this routine. At first, you may not be able to do all of these exercises in twenty minutes. Don't worry about that! Simply choose several of them, and as your strength increases, you will be able to add on until you have mastered these as well.

I must stress, however, that a twenty-minute routine is no substitute for the regular Super Callanetics one-hour regimen. These are only designed to be substitutes when you are severely pressed for time.

WARM-UPS

1. The Waist-Away Stretch • 100 REPS EACH SIDE

2. Underarm Tightener • 100 REPS

STOMACH

3. Sit Up and Curl Down • FOLLOW DIRECTIONS CAREFULLY!

LEGS

4. Pelvic-Wave Leg Strengthener • 3 SETS

5. Hamstring Stretch #2—Bent Leg • HOLD FOR A COUNT OF 50

Try to do this with your heel underneath your barre.

BUTTOCKS—OUTER THIGHS—HIPS
6. Standing Out to the Side • 100 REPS

THE ENTIRE BODY
7. Open and Close • 50 REPS

STRETCHES
8. Spine Stretch • HOLD FOR A COUNT OF 100 ON EACH SIDE

PELVIS—FRONT and INNER THIGHS
9. Pelvic Rotation • 20 REPS OF A FULL CIRCLE TO THE RIGHT, AND THEN 20 REPS OF A FULL CIRCLE TO THE LEFT
10. Inner-Thigh Squeeze • 100 REPS

The one exercise I always do whenever I can, even while standing and talking to someone, is the Standing Out to the Side. Most people don't have a clue I'm doing it. If you do attempt this exercise, make sure you do an equal amount on each side, for this exercise works so fast, your buttocks will become lopsided if you favour one side over the other. How embarrassing this would be in a tight dress or tight trousers!

If it's appropriate, I'll also try to do the The Waist-Away Stretch and the Underarm Tightener when other people are around. They usually join in with enthusiasm! Play around with these—you will soon be quite surprised what you can accomplish (and where!). Your balance will soon improve so drastically that you won't have to worry about holding onto anything for support.

A Final Message

Not long ago an elderly man who does Super Callanetics regularly said to me, 'Callan, don't use up your energy trying to explain to people what the difference is between Super Callanetics and other exercises. There's simply no way they will understand until they've done Super Callanetics themselves. Just tell them it's like the difference between the postman and a fax machine. Both of them will deliver a letter, but you can get that letter so much faster with a fax. And there's no damage to it.'

I like that analogy. Super Callanetics has offered so many people an incredible opportunity to take their body strength beyond what they would have classified as their limitations, without stress or strain—no damage to it. It is such a wonderful feeling to know that your very own body can accomplish incredible feats that you never even thought possible.

And so I will continue to take advantage of all that Super Callanetics has to offer, along with the thousands of other people who have used it to transform their bodies. And the reason I can do so with complete confidence is because I have a guarantee that every time I do Super Callanetics, I know that not only will I have a tighter body when I have completed the routine, but I will not ever have to worry about injuring myself. Super Callanetics is a more efficient way to maintain—in less time—the incredible results you already will have obtained from mastering the one-hour program. And Super Callanetics provides an incredible challenge for those of you who have trained your muscles so well. Even more important than your physical transformation will be your *mental* transformation—the glowing look that accompanies self-confidence and an improved self-image.

Callanetics

The revolutionary
all-over deep muscle exercise
system devised by

CALLAN PINCKNEY

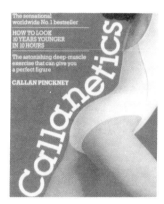

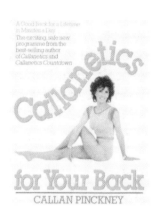

Please send me _____ copy/ies of

☐ CALLANETICS @ £7.99 paperback

☐ CALLANETICS COUNTDOWN @ £7.99 paperback

☐ CALLANETICS FOR YOUR BACK @ £7.99 paperback

Post order to: **Murlyn Services Ltd, P.O. Box 50, Harlow, Essex CM17 0D2**

Mrs/Miss/Ms/Mr_____ Initials_____

Address_____

_____ Postcode_____

Enclosed cheque/PO *(payable to Ebury Press)* for £_____

or debit my ACCESS/VISA Card No. _____

for £_____ Expiry Date_____

Signature_____ Telephone Number_____

STOP PRESS! We also have a telephone HOTLINE for Access/Visa cardholders.
Just phone 0279-27203

OFFER OPEN IN GREAT BRITAIN (INCLUDING NORTHERN IRELAND) ONLY. POSTAGE AND PACKING FREE. Books should arrive within 28 days of receipt of your order. If not entirely satisfied, return (in same packaging and condition as received) with a covering letter within 7 days. This book is available from good booksellers. It is subject to availability at time of ordering.

WHAT EVERY BODY NEEDS

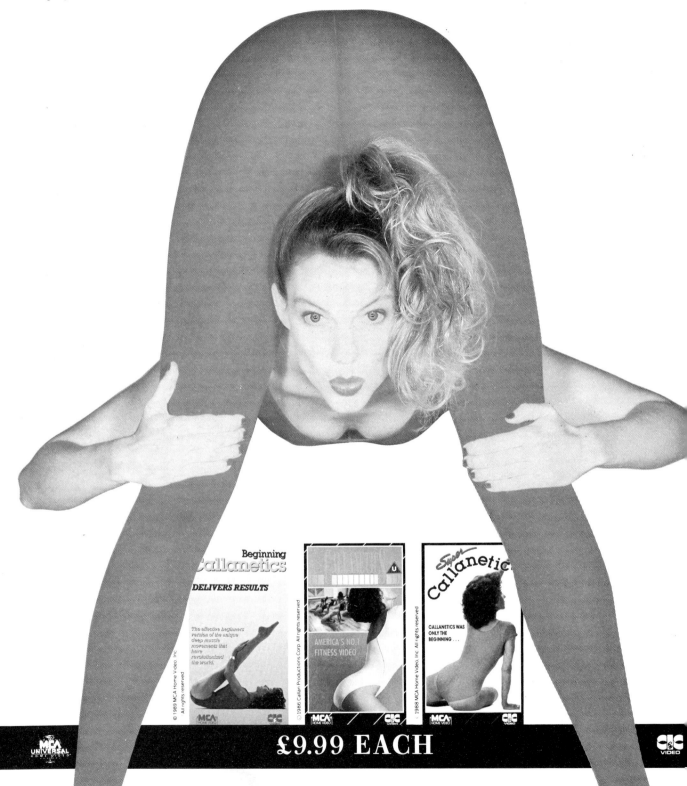